The Erotics of Cutting Grass

01 02 03 04 05 29 28 27 26 25

Caitlin Press Inc.
3375 Ponderosa Way
Qualicum Beach, BC V9K 2J8
www.caitlinpress.com

Text and cover design by Vici Johnstone

Printed in Canada

Caitlin Press Inc. acknowledges financial support from the Government of Canada and the Canada Council for the Arts, and the Province of British Columbia through the British Columbia Arts Council and the Book Publisher's Tax Credit.

Canada Council for the Arts Conseil des Arts du Canada BRITISH COLUMBIA ARTS COUNCIL Funded by the Government of Canada Canada

The erotics of cutting grass : reflections on a well-loved life / by Kate Braid.
Braid, Kate, author
Canadiana 20240467205 | ISBN 9781773861623 (softcover)
LCSH: Braid, Kate. | LCSH: Authors, Canadian—20th century—Biography. | LCSH: Older women— Canada—Biography. | LCSH: Aging—Humor. | CSH: Authors, Canadian (English)—20th century— Biography. | LCGFT: Autobiographies. | LCGFT: Essays.
LCC PS8553.R2585 Z46 2025 | DDC C811/.54—dc23

the erotics of cutting grass

Reflections on a Well-Loved Life

Kate Braid

Caitlin Press 2025

Contents

Wising Up

Wonder Woman a.k.a. Emily Carr

When I was fourteen, I met Rima. Not a real person, but a character in a novel called *Green Mansions*, published in 1927 by British writer, W.H. Hudson. I'm not sure how I got hold of the book. Although I was already an avid reader, we had few books in our house so I must have borrowed it from the Bookmobile, a small miracle of a bus that showed up in our neighbourhood every few weeks, packed with books free for the borrowing.

What I remember, looking back, is that *Green Mansions'* heroine, Rima, lived in the South American jungle in fabulous independence. Rima could survive where others could not, weaving her dresses from spiders' webs, eating wild berries and fruits, hurting no creature, living exactly as she wished. I was a girl raised in the 1950s to aim for marriage, children, and obedience to her husband. Full stop. So Rima's independence was a shocking idea and I realized I wanted that too, though I didn't tell anyone. It felt too precious a dream, and definitely not acceptable. After all, Rima was a wild girl, "a savage," as the male protagonist of the book calls her.

I guess you could say I followed through on my dream to be like Rima, though I ended up not in a South American jungle, but in a British Columbian West Coast forest of two-by-fours. In the 1970s and '80s I became a construction labourer, apprentice and journey carpenter, eventually running my own renovation business and teaching construction at the BC Institute of Technology.

But it wasn't all as easy or straightforward as that list might suggest. Certainly, at the time, getting into construction work had an aspect of resistance to it that I recognized from *Green Mansions*. Sort of like weaving your dresses out of spiders' webs, no one in the 1970s had heard of a woman doing blue-collar work. I got into it by accident, because I was running out of money at the time, so it was pure bonus to discover I loved building: having a concrete product at the end of each day, being outdoors, using my body, feeling fit and strong, getting paid well.

But I was being closely and critically watched. Most women looked at me with what felt like awe. Most men shook their heads in disbelief. None had ever worked with a woman before. There were many decent men on that first job and on the ones that followed, but there were others who clearly didn't want me there. Every day I was keenly aware I was less than a minority; I was a token, and life on the job would be easier without having to include "The Girl." It was lonely.

Then a crazy thing happened. I was poking around a used bookstore in the city and found a comic book called *The Adventures of Wonder Woman*. The cover alone was shocking: a strong woman (gorgeous and skimpily clad, but nonetheless) flying dramatically through the air, rescuing people. And she looked happy to do it! I'd never heard of *Wonder Woman*, but given that people on the island where I lived and worked often looked at me as I were indeed some rare form of "wonder woman," I bought the comic and by the time I got off the ferry and home that afternoon, had read it three times. Yes! Women could be "weird" and still do the so-called impossible!

Wonder Woman became my mentor, my inspiration. At the time, I was living alone in a plywood cabin in the woods and I always kept one of her comic books on the table so I could catch a glimpse of her every night as I came in the door from work. Just the image of her was enough for now; I wasn't alone.

One year later I moved to Vancouver, partly to move in with my boyfriend and his son, partly to finish my thesis on women in non-traditional work in BC—a subject I'd chosen so I could have an excuse to find and talk to other tradeswomen around the province. On International Women's Day in 1979, I helped another woman, a printer, organize a workshop on women in non-traditional work and in this way connected with some of the few other women who did trades work. There were about ten of us in that first workshop—carpenters, welders, a boilermaker, electrician, avionics mechanic and others, all thrilled to find each other. We formed a group called Women in Trades so we could meet on a regular basis and keep each other's courage up.

Still, all my working time was spent with men who, if they weren't directly opposed, didn't exactly approve of me being there. I loved construction work with a passion, but the culture of the workplace, the way men interacted and how I was somehow always "different," had me seriously wondering if this job was really worth the emotional pressure. It was too hard always being the only woman.

And then I met Emily Carr. Not in person, of course—she died in 1945—but in her work. One Saturday afternoon while wandering idly through the Vancouver Art Gallery, I saw one of her paintings of forest.

You can't live in BC and not run across pictures, postcards and paintings by Emily Carr, but I'd always dismissed them as dark and uninteresting. Not this time. This time, after two years spent happily living in the woods and handling wood at work every day, all day, I had to sit down to catch my breath and take a closer look. This woman had captured the spirit of trees. Emily knew!

I started paying closer attention to her paintings, and then reading her books. Emily's story almost paralleled my own. In the first half of the twentieth century, everyone "knew" women couldn't be serious painters—a bit like how, in the second half of the century, they "knew" women couldn't be carpenters. The women of Emily's generation might be allowed a few pretty oils as recreation, a way to pass a quiet Sunday afternoon, but paint as a professional artist? Unimaginable! Everyone knew women couldn't do that!

Emily Carr bucked that tide. She even turned down a marriage proposal because she knew marriage and children wouldn't allow her to take her artwork seriously.

This rang more than a few bells with me. But what moved me most was the tenacity of her vision. No one encouraged this woman to paint, even her family. In this, I had one clear advantage. Not until the end of her life did Emily's family barely acknowledge her painting. ("Nice picture frames," one sister said.) But once I'd got up the courage to announce to my parents, carefully, in a letter, that I was now a construction worker, there was a long silence and then, for Christmas, the present of a pair of grey wool, genuine "worker" socks with a red stripe on the top, and a T-shirt that announced, "The best man for the job may be a woman." It was okay!

But Emily carried on without any support, starting her career with a major trip up the BC coast, a white woman alone, painting the Indigenous villages and totem poles she loved. Back in her hometown, Victoria, when she tried to sell those paintings, people weren't interested in this strange new subject matter, let alone the weird woman who'd painted them.

This too, felt familiar. After years of having almost given up, Emily's journals, *Hundreds and Thousands,* document her intense struggle to be a painter after 1927 when she'd become so broke, so discouraged, she'd virtually given up painting and was raising dogs and running a boarding house to make a living. But in that year, on a trip east where her art was to be shown in a display of Indigenous and West Coast painting, she'd met Lawren Harris and the Group of Seven. During that visit Harris said to her, "You are one of us," and his encouragement gave her the strength to carry on. Even then, Emily had more than a hint of the early feminist about her. In 1937, she wrote, "I am also glad that I am showing these men that women can hold up their end."

It was Emily's story as I read it in her books and paintings that gave me the courage to stay in construction for many more years, and to become an activist in the trades. It was Emily, unafraid to march down Government Street with a monkey on her shoulder and pushing a baby carriage to carry the clay she needed for her pots (how practical!) who inspired me to carry on, to speak up. She also inspired me to take my own writing more seriously, to keep up a habit of making daily notes of my building days, trying to understand the strange culture of construction. Eventually I wrote several books of poetry and prose about my experience of being a woman in the trades, then a biography of Emily, called *Emily Carr: Rebel Artist,* and a book of poems in response to her paintings, *To This Cedar Fountain,* and again, a book of poems about an imaginary journey she might have taken with my other inspiration, Georgia O'Keeffe, *Inward to the Bones: Georgia O'Keeffe's Journey with Emily Carr.* Each of them was another way to spend time in the company of these strong women.

I'd always found it interesting that Emily's favourite character on the northern BC totem poles had been D'Sonoqua, also known as Zunoqua—Wild Woman of the Woods. Later, I discovered that the Wild Woman is a powerful character in many cultures: she's Sequana in the Celtic traditions I trace from; and Artemis, Protector of the Amazons (also known as Diana, or the Virgin), to the Greeks. There's a whole book about her, *Women Who Run With the Wolves: Myths and Stories of the Wild Woman Archetype,* by Clarissa Pinkola Estés. Published in 1992, it was a best seller for a record number of weeks. Clearly, I wasn't the only one interested in Wild Women! I put a postcard picture of Artemis on one side of my writing desk, D'Sonoqua on the other, and carried on.

Meanwhile, Women in Trades groups were forming across Canada and in 1980 we had our first national meeting. The organization would go on, nationally then internationally. There is no doubt, the support and companionship of other women in trades kept me going, and all along, I kept *Hundreds and Thousands* by my side.

Still, after fifteen years, I was just too lonely and finally did leave the trade. But I was lucky, I had another passion—writing.

I enrolled in the Master of Fine Arts program at the University of British Columbia (UBC), and began teaching creative writing as well as writing my own books.

Along the way, I went back and reread *Green Mansions*. I was horrified to find that, far from being the heroine of the book, Rima, my childhood inspiration, was a minor figure, the love interest to a very traditional white British "hero" who is blatantly racist, sexist and condescending. Worse, by the end of the book, Rima is murdered—burned alive—by local people afraid of her and her independence in the jungle. Clearly, independent wild women were not allowed, were to be feared and eliminated at all costs.

But by then it didn't matter that I'd got the story wrong. It was the story as I understood it as a fourteen-year-old, as I *needed* to understand it, that gave me the courage to resist tradition and follow my own "wild" path.

Incidentally, I found out, years later that the concept and comic of *Wonder Woman* had been started by a man, a Jungian psychologist named William Moulton Marston, in 1941. It was wartime, the time of Rosie the Riveter when women were being called into shipyards and factories, workplaces they'd never been allowed before but where now, with so many men at war, there was such a desperate labour shortage that even women would do.

When it was first published, the image of Wonder Woman, the cartoon character, became so popular and there was such demand, that three years later Marston hired a nineteen-year-old named Joye Hummel (later Joye Murchison Kelly) to help him. She wrote seventy scripts for and with him, though her name appeared on none of them and in 1947 she married and quit her job to stay home. Hummel's role was only discovered in 2014 when another writer, Jill Lepore, researching a book to be called *The Secret History of Wonder Woman,* found out about her.

Hummel's son told a newspaper reporter that when Dr. Marston started the comic, "He was not writing just an adventure book. He hoped that the young women who read the stories would be inspired to study and enter the world and have confidence they could accomplish things." Clearly, in at least one case, it succeeded. And judging by the wild success of the Wonder Woman character ever since, mine wasn't an isolated case. Wonder Woman almost instantly became an archetypical figure in popular culture. There's even a Wonder Woman Day—October 21.

Rima, Wonder Woman, Emily Carr—all of them remind women and all others who've been "put in their places" for too long, that letting our stories be told is powerful, telling them ourselves is something we can do for each other, a way to pass our courage along. Lately there's increasing speculation that one reason for the growing strength of women's movements such as #MeToo, and the numbers of well-known men being held accountable for sexual harassment, is that women (and others) can now connect quickly and easily on social media to let each other know we're not alone. "That happened to me, too," is a powerful tool that can *en-courage*—give courage—to others, and so bring about change.

Emily Carr would agree. On December 20, 1940, she wrote in her journal, "I don't suppose we know from moment to moment what trivial happening is going to develop into something big or is just going to snuff right out. Maybe it is a sentence in a book or a statement by someone on the radio, or a true start, like a flight or a flower or a bird, the alive in us being caught up by the alive in the universe."

His Other Mother

One of the few things I'd always felt quite sure of was that although I might eventually find a partner, which I did, in John, I never wanted kids. So when I fell in love with this tall, quiet man, I was surprised, the second time I slept over at his co-op house, when he introduced me the next morning to a serious-looking child with big eyes.

"I'd like you to meet Kevin," he said. "My son."

Kevin was seven. Did I say I'd been clear from the start that I never wanted children? As the eldest of six, I'd had lots of experience with young ones. My job had always been to "look after the kids" and I'd known that after all that diaper-changing and cooking and minding, I wasn't at all interested in having my own children. I'd done that.

Still, I figured I'd just see where this relationship *à trois* might go.

Over the next several months, the three of us started doing things together, starting with small things like a swim in the local pool, then an afternoon's fishing trip, and a few months later, a long weekend spent fishing and camping on the Broken Islands off the coast of Vancouver Island. That was where it really sank in that, though Kevin may have been only seven, he was a person with skills of his own. At one point, all of us were dangling our lines in the water. John and I hadn't had a nibble between us so when Kevin pulled up his second fish in short order, I asked casually, "How do you do that?"

Looking very serious, he said, "I think like a fish."

Amazing! It changed my attitude to fishing—and to Kevin.

Still, when John and I made the decision to move in together, with Kevin, I was a bit non-plussed at inheriting a seven-year-old. At least he wasn't a baby. I'd have no diapers to change or midnight feedings and, best of all, he could talk. Plus, I loved his dad.

To tell the truth, it was a bit odd becoming a stepmother, an instant mother. This was 1978 and I had never even heard of anyone else who'd done it. So following my grandfather's advice that, "Everything you need is in the library," I headed to the local library where I found exactly one book on step-parenting, and it was fiction. Today there are books and columns and websites and self-help groups but in 1978 there was nothing.

Our first issue was my name. Kevin's birth mother was still very much in the picture so it wasn't as if I was a "real" mother. Kevin spent every second weekend with his birth mother, so what should he call me? "Stepmother" reminded me of every scary fairy tale I'd ever read. (Which made me wonder, why were there no evil stepfathers?) In the end we decided, Kevin and I, that I would be simply "Kate" because that was my name, and within a few months, Kevin's birth mum was more than generous when she started to call me his co-mother.

But then what? How do you act with a stepson? This was a whole new world. Somehow the word "step" implied "one-down, lesser," and that wasn't the kind of relationship I wanted at all. What kind or degree of authority should I wield? What rights did I have? What rights, the child?

It got more complicated when, soon after we moved in

together, John took a job that required long trips into isolated parts of Canada that had no telephone connections. (This was long before cellphones.) So Kevin, this little stranger, and I, were on our own for weeks at a time.

Slowly, we worked it out, mostly when his dad was away. Really, it was Kevin who let me know how he wanted to be treated and if it made sense—which it usually did—I'd go along with it. I remember one incident when he and his best friend, Eddy, were tearing through the house, yelling. They were playing, but I figured it wasn't okay because: a) my mother never let us yell in the house, and, b) I didn't like the noise. This was the first time I clearly heard my mother's voice coming out of my mouth.

"Don't yell in the house!" I yelled at the two kids as they raced past me. Eddy promptly disappeared out the back door, but Kevin lingered, looking at me with those large, brown eyes—could it be—a little reproachfully?

He stopped perfectly still, unintimidated by my Adult (I'd been aiming for Mother) Voice.

"Very well, Kate," he said slowly and deliberately, then turned and with great dignity, walked out the door. The message was clear: he would obey, but I'd shown far less grace in this exchange than he. After getting over my shock, I almost laughed aloud. *Okay kid, I get it,* I thought. *We can do this.*

There were other learning times—and I say, "learning," from my own perspective because I was immersed in a crash course in step-parenting. I'm not sure if Kevin was learning the same things, though. Like the time when he didn't like what I'd made for supper. I'd insisted from Day One of living together that the three of us would eat suppers together. It had been an ironclad rule in my childhood house, and I saw in it now my mother's wisdom about how to keep a busy family connected—by spending at least one hour a day joined over the dinner table. So John and Kevin and I were having dinner one night when Kevin complained about the soup. John and I took turns cooking and it had been my turn to make supper—this night, pea soup and salad. But I must have had a bad day because I was unusually brusque; I swept the filled spoon out of Kevin's mouth, splashing pea soup liberally across the table, and announced, "That's what's for supper. If you don't want to eat it, fine. But that's *all* there is."

Kevin, much calmer than me, pushed himself deliberately away from the table and went into the living room to play. I was instantly sorry, almost ashamed, but what could I do? John and I finished our meal in silence and as I washed the dishes I stole surreptitious glances into the living room to see if the child was showing any signs of hunger yet. No? Regret? Not that either. He did his homework and finally, just before bed, I caved.

"Would you like a snack?"

Both of us knew I was apologizing, but Kevin said calmly, "No, thank you," and returned to what he'd been doing. He was showing that same sense of—what? Not haughtiness. He wasn't sneering. He was… above that. I think "principled" is the word. I was figuring out that I could trust this kid. He had a certain grace. I'd been right, if a bit extreme, in holding the line on "Eat what's in front of you," but he'd been right too, to refuse and take the consequences.

We had no more conflicts over suppertime, and within a year or two Kevin took on his share of cooking, though one adult helped him prepare the meals when it was his turn. Until one afternoon I came home from work and he was poring over a cookbook, about to make his first pesto sauce all by himself.

At the time, the child was having trouble in school, getting into a lot of fights. Which meant that one day—again, when John was away—Kevin was sent home early from school. I was in construction at the time but not working that day so I was there when he arrived home. What was I supposed to do now? Clearly, it wasn't okay to get into fights at school. But isn't this when a father or mother steps up?

But there was no "real" mother or father around, so I took a deep breath and said, "You know it's not okay to fight."

"Kate," he said patiently, as if explaining something difficult. "I'm one of the biggest boys in the class, so all the other boys have to prove how tough they are by picking on me. I *have* to fight them."

Of course. Why hadn't I thought of that? Still, I felt obliged to give him a short talk on non-violence, and we parted amicably. There were other problems too, like the time he got so angry at his French teacher that he swept everything off the teacher's desk and stalked out of the classroom. It was only later that we'd find out the real problem of those years—that the child was dyslexic. He had a reading disability that made it difficult to keep up to the reading skills of most of the other kids in his classes, which left him embarrassed, and angry.

Still, when he went to high school I was dazzled by some of the projects he chose to work on, including a report on a woman's right to free access to abortion. Could I have had some effect on his development after all? How much was me, how much his deeply egalitarian father and how much was pure Kevin? Watching him go through school was like watching a flower open—ah, this is who he is! And this! I liked him. Clearly, I respected him. Is this how "real parents" felt?

—

When Kevin was thirty-seven, married, and working as the administrator for a United Nations peacekeeping agency, he and his wife phoned us from New York to tell us they had just had a baby daughter. And the strangest thing happened; every cell in my body realigned and I *was* a grandmother. I, who had never wanted my own kids, was profoundly changed. As if grandparenting is not merely a role, but a hormonal change. And for the next few years it was me, the step-grandmother, not John, the "real" grandfather, who constantly pushed for us to go to New York to visit.

"But she's just a baby," John would say after we'd returned from yet another visit. "She can't even talk." But that was the point. It was this baby I wanted to see, to smell, to be with, to hold. I was her grandmother, no "step" about it.

They called her Zlata, a Ukrainian name from her mother's side of the family, meaning Golden. One night when we were visiting (again) in NY, I volunteered to babysit while her parents and grandfather were out, but the child wouldn't settle. She'd always had trouble falling asleep, but on this night she was particularly niggly. I tried walking her, singing to her, rocking her, putting her down and leaving her to cry, walking her some more.... Finally, as a last resort, I stopped everything, laid her in her bed and began to recite poetry: a W.B. Yeats poem, "The Second Coming."

"Turning and turning in the widening gyre," I began, "The falcon cannot hear the falconer." Perhaps it was the iambic pentametre of the piece, its regular rhythms and rhyme, perhaps she was merely exhausted, but the child promptly fell asleep. She was a poet! In fact, as she grew up, she became an avid reader and excellent writer and we sometimes joke about how in many ways she's more like me, a writer, than anyone else in the family. When Zlata was about ten, every student in her class had to draw up a family tree and the teacher said, "Zlata, you've made a mistake. You've drawn in three grandmothers."

"But that's right," the child said. "I have three grandmothers."

I was official!

~

I may never have wanted to be a mother, but I had, still have, a particular relation first to Kevin and then to his daughter that I can't put my finger on. I always deferred to the "authority" of Kevin's birth mum and dad in making the big decisions about his life (though I can't think of any time we disagreed), but increasingly I knew I had a role in his, and now in his daughter's life. What's the name: Caregiver? Friend? Confidante? Supporter? I decided the name doesn't matter. My job is to love them. Okay, to blatantly adore them, but from a slightly one-step-away position. That slight distance of not being blood-related never felt chilling. Indeed, it was precious. *Is* precious. It means Kevin and Zlata and I can talk about things that might have been a bit scarier with birth parents or grandparents. Kevin knew, and Zlata now knows, they have another friend besides their parents, an ally, a boon companion who loves them madly, who is always available.

But the real gift has been for me. I have not only a child, but thanks to my son and my daughter-in-law, also a grandchild, and I didn't even have to go through all that messy baby stuff. I am profoundly grateful.

Me and Pablo Casals

Some time after Kevin had left home to travel and go to university, I began to think of learning the cello. Nobody knew I'd always yearned to play cello—not even me. When I was young, the only instrument whose sound I actively hated was cello's first cousin, the violin. I think, looking back, it was because violin, cello, viola, guitar—all of them, for me, were the most emotional of instruments. And during my adolescence, I didn't want anything to do with emotion.

Years later, during the course of researching for a book of poems about the painters Georgia O'Keeffe and Emily Carr, I was driving home on a warm mid-summer evening. A pink and gold sunset blanketed both sides of the highway as CBC radio played three cellists—Mstislav Rostropovich, Yo Yo Ma and Pablo Casals—comparing their treatments of Bach's First Cello Suite.

I'd never heard of Bach's cello suites and at the time, I didn't like the music of Bach almost as much as I didn't like the sound of cello. So why was I suddenly so overwhelmed that I had to pull the car over to listen more closely, and to weep? How was it that people could express so much emotion with music, especially with that instrument I'd mostly ignored, the cello.

Afterward, I shook myself, told myself not to be ridiculous, but I thought, "This is Georgia's music." Months later I found out that Casals' version of Bach's Cello Suites was indeed O'Keeffe's favourite music, something she played often for herself in the desert.

By then I'd bought Rostropovich's version, and was playing it regularly. I found there's a time for the cello suites: usually when I'm in the car, when I'm travelling through wild and beautiful countryside, or at night, when I'm in a certain mood, a little bit spacey, a little bit blue....

Then I discovered another cellist, Jacqueline du Pré. Someone at the record store recommended her CD and I bought it, a double disc that included the Elgar Concerto and the Dvorak. I'd never heard of either. When I got home and put it on, Dvorak was up first. Orchestra? Very nice. When du Pré hit the first chords on her cello, I happened to be walking through the living room. I say "hit" the chords. This woman didn't just play; she attacked, she tore, she trembled so wildly into that first chord that—as if someone had whacked me at the knees—I buckled and sat down. Breathless.

I thought, *This is silly*. I may *wish* music hit me like this, but it never does. Or never has before, except for that one time on the road....

I stood up. Du Pré fell onto another phrase. I sat down. She stopped, I stood up. She played, I sat down. Like a puppet for the next several minutes, I was subject to her strings. It's a cliché, but I'd never heard anything like it: terrible passion, heart, terror, fury, love all in one place. I listened to those two discs for the rest of the day, the next day, and to some extent, regularly since.

~

A few years after that, when I was teaching at the local university, I had a brief chat with a student as we waited for class to begin. She told me she'd just taken up the violin.

"How wonderful!" I said and meant it. "If there's one thing I wish I'd done," I said idly, "it's to learn to play the cello."

"Why don't you?" she replied.

I hate it when people ask that question. I knew instantly I was defeated. Why didn't I indeed? We looked each other in the eye and I said, "It's not because I'm too old. . . ." I thought a minute. Why was it then? "I don't have time." Ah yes, that great excuse for everything.

My student said she only practises ten minutes a day, and looked at me again. I fluttered a bit, called the class to order, and the next afternoon, watching the bearded guy ahead of me make copies of music at the Xerox machine, was amazed to hear myself ask, "You wouldn't know anyone in town who teaches cello, would you?" Just joking, sort of.

"Yes," he said. "My cousin, Krystal. She specializes in teaching adults." He introduced himself, a trombone player. "Did you know," he said as I headed back to my office, "musicians say among themselves that cello is the hardest instrument to play?"

I didn't want to know, but what does one do when faced with the powers of synchronicity? I phoned Krystal. She said I was not insane. She said adults *can* learn the cello, told me there was a group of adults she knew, all just learning cello, who got together once a month to play. She told me where to rent an instrument.

~

But I'm not so easy; I delayed. This was nuts. I was fifty-three years old, couldn't read a note of music, had never played an instrument in my life except to pluck at a guitar one year, and now I wanted to play Bach—one of the more difficult composers—on a cello, one of the most difficult instruments? Ridiculous.

Until a friend told me she had just received a diagnosis of breast cancer and had to have a full mastectomy, both breasts removed.

Until my breasts ached all the day of her surgery as I drove to class.

Until I thought, *Something beautiful should be happening while something so terrible is going on.* And I bowed to coincidence. While my friend underwent a double mastectomy, I rented a cello. At least one beautiful thing would be happening in the world while a woman gave up her breasts to cancer.

In the music store, a pleasant man with a European accent showed me an instrument. It looked fine to me but what should I be looking for, anyway?

"It's new," he said. I did know from my brief telephone conversation with Krystal that "new" in stringed instruments isn't always good. But what difference does it make? I told the man I had never played an instrument before, but I really wanted to play cello. I wanted to play like Jacqueline du Pré.

He said, "Just a minute, there's another instrument that came back a few minutes ago," and showed me another. It was more beaten up but when he asked if I could wait ten minutes while he cleaned it for me, I said yes, because in theory (at least, the only theory I knew), an older instrument sounds better than a new one. Sort of like people?

All the way home, I had a stupid grin on my face but once I got there and pulled the instrument out of its case, then the bow, I was almost afraid. So I took a deep breath and "played." I pulled the bow across the strings, one string. Look Ma, no hands! It sounded divine.

A cello, or at least this one, was smaller than I'd expected. A humble-looking instrument. I had thought cellos must be—are—huge. How else could all that power come from such a small box, small heart? But no, its wooden body fit so easily between my knees that I could almost cover it, surround it, embrace it. And yes, it sounded like the voice of a god. When I put it back in its case, I put it in backward.

I had a lot to learn.

John said I might have to cut a hole in the floor to brace the long pin it sat on, and I realized it had never crossed my mind that a cello would touch the floor. In my mind, it hovered in air, was magical. Then he asked, "Who are you going to play with?" That hadn't crossed my mind either. He said, "That's what musicians do, they play together." John plays guitar; he knows.

But that wasn't what I wanted. I had a vision of myself (I blush to say this now) that was like a photo of Pablo Casals we'd seen on a TV special the week before. It was taken from the back, Casals seated with his cello inside an old stone tower filled with shadows. The light from a single window shone down on him, hunched forward intensely as he played, his instrument, the cello almost invisible as he encircled it, embraced it, creating magic. That's what I wanted too: to be alone with my cello, making divine music.

When I told the people in my life about my new project, they were, to put it mildly, surprised. My father said, "Why cello?" A friend asked, "Why don't you join a choir? It's easier." Most of my friends, though mystified, were happy for me. Perhaps it showed that I was still alive, that to be fifty-three and outrageous, is a good sign. It was my mother who most surprised me. She said, "I always wanted to play the piano." So did the woman selling fish at Safeway. I told them both to go for it.

For the next few days I seemed to be grinning all the time. This new project might be insane, but it sure felt good.

I phoned Krystal and made an appointment for a lesson. She worked at a local academy of music, an easy halfway stop between work and home. It felt, again, as if the gods had laid out a glistening *capriccio* carpet that I'd just stepped onto. I was flying!

On the first day that I arrived at the school, it felt like arriving for a baptism, a wedding, as I carried my cello down a long corridor peppered with the luscious sound of scales and violins and music—like the smells of something delicious cooking. To Studio 18.

I knocked.

The woman who opened the door was about my age, an old hippie in a multicoloured skirt, loose shirt and a bright shawl. Her blonde hair, pulled back in a loose ponytail, looked naturally curly. She was shy and quiet and at first we fumbled around each other as if on a first date. She used language I'd never heard before: the pin, open D scale, descending fifths, as if my date spoke with a foreign accent. I felt awkward as I undid zippers, pulled the wooden vessel from its case, then the bow. Krystal didn't even look at the bow.

"Hold your instrument like this," she said firmly. "Your hands, so. No, your baby finger must be curled too, as if over an orange, a lemon." To illustrate, she pushed a neon green tennis ball up into the natural-looking curve of her left hand. It looked easy but when I tried it, my little finger was stiff, straight, white with effort. She gave me exercises for my ignorant fingers, put little blue sticky circles on the neck of my cello (*my* cello!) to show where my number one and number four fingers (number one? number four?) should go, then my thumb. I placed my hands. I plucked a string.

"A," she said, "This is A string." My fingertips hurt. My baby finger lay flat, rigid, trembling. Impatient, I grabbed it with my right hand, curved it, let go. It fell flat again. I plucked. Again. "That's a descending A," she said, then, "Do you want to play a tune?"

Did I? I was ravenous for tunes. I was ravenous to sound like you-know-who. Together, one note at a time, we picked out, "Baa Baa Black Sheep." I was playing the cello.

At my lesson the following week, Krystal told me the most important thing was to practise every day. So far I'd missed twice and today, after a nap, I would indeed practise. I bowed my head as if to hide. What was this strange feeling of hesitation at approaching the cello? As if approaching something holy, something I might hurt.

Listening to me practise on any day would hurt my own ears and those of anyone within hearing distance, but I'd be on my way to music! Every day that week, I did my left-hand finger exercises: clip fingers together in fast Os, play as if all the combinations of my fingers are scissors, teach them to move independently of each other, to be strong.

Two weeks later, Krystal let me use the bow. Like a real cellist. She instructed me to move it very carefully, very slowly, with two hands, watching how it sat on the strings as I gently pulled it across. Meanwhile, inside, I was a raging barbarian, warrior woman, one handed, swinging my bow like a sword across the strings, producing streams of music. I couldn't wait!

I slowed down when I heard the not-so-pleasant effect. Slow sounded better. I pulled my bow across each of the strings, and then I played a song. I'd abandoned "Baa Baa Black Sheep." "Hot Cross Buns" was now my specialty. "Hot Cross Buns" was my only tune. It didn't matter that most people would have thought it a child's ditty; "Hot Cross Buns" was my anthem. That, and a single scale.

"Open D," Krystal said. I played it up and down and up and down and....

Practice was now no problem. At home I only practised ten or fifteen minutes at a time because my options were so limited. Krystal was right; "Hot Cross Buns," even on all four strings, and open D scale on two, could get a bit tedious. Especially when I squealed, which was often. But making time—always a problem for other things like marking student papers—was suddenly no problem at all. As I waited for the kettle to boil, while I heated soup, when I took a break from anything else, time was suddenly boundless, everywhere!

The best, the thing that drew me back, that felt like meeting a lover each time, was that the cello resonated in my chest. Extraordinary. My whole body played cello. A friend who plays violin once told me the musician's body is another part of the resonating cavity—body, flesh and bone and blood and wooden instrument all together. Now I remembered that wood gets better with age. And the body? I noticed it the first time I practised at home. As if *we*, the instrument and I, were singing together.

Two weeks later I woke up deaf in my left ear. Or at least, with all sound muffled as if my ear were full of water. The doctor said I must have a blocked eustachian tube, said "infected sinus," said "allergies, decongestants, tubes if it doesn't clear...."

How ironic. After hearing the cello resonate in my chest, to lose my hearing! At night I dreamed I was trying to weave cello sounds together to make the "ow" sound in "How."

Sometimes at the end of a lesson, Krystal and I had been playing a couple of (very simple) tunes together. While she played the Teacher line on four strings and I played Student on two, I heard music—almost beautiful! But after my hearing loss, I couldn't hit even the few notes I knew. I was always flat or sharp or missing the note entirely, losing my place. It was almost as if—I hardly dared think it—almost as if I couldn't hear properly. As of course, I couldn't. The deafness was in my left ear, my cello-side ear. But I had another ear, not so far away! It was something about balance, the balance of sounds in my head....

Once when I had played particularly badly and the lesson was mercifully over, I packed my cello, opened the door to flee—and there was a boy, maybe ten, standing facing me with his cello by his side, waiting for his lesson. He'd heard me! It was like facing myself as a child, the ghost of what was lost, the young cello player I never was, and now perhaps, never could be.

But as I walked back to the car, I thought, *No. I may fumble and struggle, but I will keep trying to find the small thread to take me back to that child.* I was determined to find her.

A few weeks later there was a report on CBC radio that

described how there's a whole surge of baby boomers taking music lessons. All of us who had worked too hard, moved too fast in our lives, were only now taking time for a deep breath, time to realize if we wanted beauty and harmony in our lives, that time was now.

I kept hoping, kept practising. One afternoon I was in the country, with doors and windows closed out of respect for my neighbours. When I opened the door to take a break, there was a doe lying in the clearing very near. Usually, deer are creatures of the early morning and dusk, skittish when they see humans. I'd never seen one so close before, and rarely during the day. This one now raised her head, looking at me calmly. For a moment we simply watched each other—creature to creature. It felt like she'd been listening to my poor strings, hearing harmony, even when it was barely there.

Two days later, back in the city, I opened a window when I began my practice and when I heard a scrabble there, looked up to see a large jay perched on the window frame. He stayed for some time as I did my best on "Au Clair de la Lune" and "My Small Waltz." At least wild creatures liked my music!

And there were moments. On pieces like "Au Clair" where I now knew the notes and was better at finding them square on, I had begun to feel the music, to put my heart into the expression. And that was wonderful. If only I could have heard it better! Something about the complexity of the strings, the sound, had gone missing.

I found that if I practised in the morning while I was more alert and physically a tiny bit stronger, I could hold my elbows, the bow, higher and it sounded better. There were precious seconds when it even sounded good, a single note, a hint of emotion....

I usually made a point of not practising when John was home, but one night after an argument I felt the need for music. I was all off key, forgot which note was where, but for the first time I understood why people go to their instruments. It felt like pouring everything that was sour inside me into the cello where it could be—was—transformed. As if I were translating chaos into something a little bit beautiful.

All the next summer I hardly practised—busy with writing and if not that, then running from one doctor to another, trying to make sense out of what had happened with my ear: Why? Why? There was still no sound on my left side, my cello side. But then it was September and I was back to teaching and marking and I didn't practise at all for two full months.

I'd almost decided to give it up. It was too hard, too discouraging to try to hear more, listen harder, ridiculous for a person with one ear to try to play an instrument, especially one I was so new at. The cello was rented until the end of October and then, my rational mind had decided, I would take it back.

But one night I felt a huge urge to play—*did* play, with great pleasure, and great pain to John's ears, I'm sure. He had never, ever complained. That night he postponed dinner until I had well and truly finished—which didn't take that long. My out-of-practice arm had quickly weakened, holding the bow up at right angles, clenching the wild animal between my legs, pressing with my soft left fingers. But I wanted it.

At the end of October I returned the cello to the rental shop. Part of me was saying, "This is right." The other part yearned desperately to make music. Of course, I still could—with my voice, especially since the cello is so beautiful partly because it sounds like a voice.

I could have joined a choir. But I didn't, not then. For lack of time? Because it wasn't my first choice?

Then—synchronicity again—I met a couple at a dinner party who ran a choir, and they invited me to join. Over the course of the next few days I met them again in the library. Then in the food store. Each time they asked again, and in the end, how could I say no, though I hadn't sung in a choir since high school?

When I went to my first practice, the group, about sixty people strong, was singing mostly gospel and soul music, which made me nervous. I'm not a churchgoer. But the music was rambunctious and full of heart, with a wonderful director who was tough but funny, who'd changed the words to some of our songs so no one could be put off, and the blended sounds we made, I had to admit, were glorious.

As I'd suspected, singing in harmony—I'm an alto—wasn't as easy as it used to be. Two ears give you two "microphones" to hear with. It's one of the reasons we're able to tell which direction sound is coming from. I had to both listen to myself to keep in pitch, and listen to the other altos as well as the rest of the choir to keep in time, all with one ear. It was a lot harder than singing with two ears, but there was something more going on. After several tunes, I became aware of feeling something odd.

It was vibration. My entire body was subtly vibrating and when I paid attention, I realized it was the physical impact of one body being literally "in harmony" with others. It wasn't the same as playing cello. It wasn't as close, as intimate, as strictly personal. These other voices weren't a rich wood hugged to my chest, whispering to me, with me. But together, these fifty-nine other voices and I were making music. We were in harmony.

It felt divine.

The Ear That Went Away

Most people, when I tell them I am profoundly deaf in one ear, nod knowingly and say, "Ah yes, all those years in construction."

But it's not so simple. When I left construction in 1995, my hearing was fine; one of the bonuses of union work was a truck that regularly came around to job sites to test our hearing. When I put down my tools, the hearing in both my ears was excellent. No, it wasn't construction.

Then one morning in February 2002, I woke up dreaming I was underwater. Even when fully awake, the feeling that my left ear was full of water stayed with me. I couldn't hear properly. I rubbed the ear, clapped the left side of my head with my hand several times, yawned over and over—still that feeling of water, and all day I felt a bit off balance. The ear irked me. What the hell was going on here? When I went to my teaching job the next day, I couldn't hear my students properly because of the noisy overhead fan I'd never noticed before, and I seemed not to be able to pick out what part of the classroom they might be speaking from.

"Just a little cold in your ear," my mother said on the phone the next morning. "It will pass in a day or two." But it didn't pass. It got worse. The first two times I went to my doctor, he looked in my ear. Nothing. He prescribed antibiotics, but those made no difference at all. The third time I went, by now truly worried, my doctor was away and the locum looked in my ears, then held a metal tuning fork up to my ears, right, then left. The sound was clearly different. When he balanced the fork on the bone behind each of my ears, again, it was different.

"I think you better get that tested," he said. He looked worried.

~

A week later I see an audiologist. I've never had my hearing tested this thoroughly before. In the middle of her office, as if plunked there by some construction giant, is a perfect little metal cabinet, a box with a door in it. It's about four feet square with a large window on the audiologist's side so—or so I figure—those of us with a touch of claustrophobia don't rush out screaming as soon as the door is closed. I quickly realize by the strange sound quality when the door shut, that this little room is soundproof, padded with something soft and silver. Inside is one chair and a pair of headphones that the audiologist asks me to put on. She goes out, closes the door and immediately reappears through the window, sitting down at her desk in front of a console I'd vaguely noticed when I walked in. She puts on her own headphones, twiddles some knobs and her voice very clearly in my right ear says, "Can you hear me?" I nod, a little unsure about all this, and she explains she'll play a series of sounds in each of my ears. All I have to do is to tell her when I stop hearing the sounds.

This should be easy, I think. So we begin. First my right ear, the clear, un-waterlogged ear. The sounds start loudly then quickly fade and I raise my index finger when I can no longer hear them. All very straightforward, practically boring, until she gets to my left ear. Then I think she's slowed down in bringing in new sounds, and she takes them away more quickly. In fact, a few times I have to look at her to see if she's doing anything at all. Maybe she's been distracted, forgotten me? But no. A quick glance and she's still there, bent over the monitors.

I know by now that something is wrong. Why is this ear taking so much longer? I cheat. I begin to watch her hands, to see when she turns knobs or pushes buttons, but she's cleverly covered them so I can't see what she's doing, or when.

Suddenly her voice comes in clearly. "I'm now going to say a few words and I want you to repeat them back to me."

No sweat. Again, she starts in my good right ear—*soldier, top, tone*—and I repeat them back, confident I have them right. Then the volume dips and there are different words but I'm certain I get them all. A third time, still quieter.

But now a strange thing happens; the sound in my right ear stops and her voice is in my left ear but there's that water feeling again, and it's hard, really hard, to hear the actual words. It isn't a problem of volume exactly. I can hear the loudness but not the letters, if you know what I mean. It's simply muffled sound.

My heart has started pounding. I suddenly realize I'm hunched over, my stomach taut, head bent, arms pulled tight to my sides. I straighten, take a deep breath. This is very, very important. My hands are clenched into two fists and I open them wide. A few minutes later they're tight again but I don't care anymore because by now the audiologist's voice is so faint, so muffled, it's like listening through a door to Mum and Dad telling secrets that I have to know. I have to know!

But I can't hear.

Then it's over. The audiologist opens the door to my little cabinet and waves me toward a chair. When I'm seated, she pulls her own chair close and shows me a piece of paper with a graph on it. At first I can't hear anything she's saying, I feel so addled. I take a deep breath. She's pointing at the graph.

"This is your right ear," she says. "You see how this line is fairly straight. You have perfectly normal, even above-average hearing in this ear."

I don't think ahead, I don't let my eyes drop to the next graph where the line looks very different. She's so calm, so matter-of-fact.

"This is your left ear," she's saying. "You can see how the sound falls off." The sound. This thin black line that represents my link to the world, to my partner's voice, to music, to bird song, this line that clearly starts at a much lower place on the graph than the right ear, then dives even further. No wonder my ear has felt full of water. It's swimming, that's all. It's just away for a while.

Now the audiologist looks at me. She's saying something but I've missed it. She says it again. "I think you should go to an ENT," she says. I frown. A what?

"An ear nose and throat specialist," she repeats. "Immediately."

I freeze. I want to smile, to cast it all off lightly, her obvious alarm. But she hasn't actually said anything bad, has she? She hasn't actually said I can't hear. When I ask, she just repeats it. "An ENT. Immediately!"

I thank her and leave—I'm on automatic now—and a few days later I'm at the office of Dr. P., an ENT specialist. Again I sit in the little silver box and again the sounds are faint and far away in my left ear and then I sit in front of the doctor with the graphs between us. Maybe now someone can tell me what the hell's going on. I've had close calls before, and I've learned my lesson. I'll be good from now on, god knows I shouldn't have been that close to the speakers at the Rolling Stones, even with the ear plugs, I'll never do that again, I promise, I promise. Now can I just go home and say I've learned my lesson? This was all a mistake and Mum was right, it will be fine in a few days?

No. When he's finished, I stand outside his office door, in shock. What does he mean, they don't know what causes it? That he can't do anything about it? What kind of medicine is that?

Over the next few days, if anything, my left ear feels as if it's settled into some deeper place, fathoms under the ocean's surface, hiding there. A good friend says, "Look for the metaphor. What are you not listening to?" She became a Christian Scientist when doctors told her that her back would, could, never heal, that she might never walk again. It was Christian Science, she now says, that healed her. "Look for the metaphor," she repeats, but me, a poet, I'm not sure what she means.

A week later I go back to the ENT, only he's on leave and this time it's another doctor, a woman, and I think maybe this is good. Women usually listen better. But when she comes in, she doesn't talk or ask me anything, she just looks for a box of Kleenex. That's odd, I think. Wouldn't she'd blow her nose before coming in? But she gives the Kleenex box to me. I take one. Is this some new therapy?

The new ENT takes a deep breath and says, "You have what we call Idiopathic Sudden Sensori-Neural Deafness. We see about ten people a month who have it, more women, more in the wintertime. We think it's caused by a virus but we're not sure. It's permanent hearing loss. The only possible treatment is a shot of…" (she names a drug starting with "p," prednisone?) "…within three days of the onset of symptoms, but even that doesn't usually work. There's nothing else we can do."

She stops here, as if I'm supposed to say something, supposed to say "thank you," but she's only taken a breath, she's still talking.

"It's very important, with any kind of deafness, that you be aware of safety issues. We need two ears to locate the source of sounds, so when you hear a horn, or a siren, or a car coming as you cross the road, you'll have no idea where that sound is coming from. Also…." and on she goes but I've stopped listening, stopped hearing. I didn't hear anything after she said "deafness." You are deaf, I tell myself. Now I understand the Kleenex. I cry.

Later, taking the bus home, I remember that when my eighty-year-old auntie found blood in her stool, the first doctor she saw dismissed it with "you're just getting old" and she said, "What kind of an attitude is that?" So she went to a second doctor who found cancer of the bowel. They operated and Auntie lived for a long time after that. Me too. I take the same "what kind of attitude is that?" position and remember my friend Russell telling me once about going to a cranial massage therapist who was enormously helpful to him at the time. "Cranial, head, ears," I think, and when I get home, phone my massage therapist who gives me a name ("Cranial-sacral") and a number and I leave a message. I also phone my chiropractor and tell the receptionist to put me on the cancellation list and sure enough, there's an appointment for three days later—a miracle—and when the cranial-sacral therapist phones me back, she has a space for me that same day.

I go. And my hearing comes back.

The chiropractor does things with my jaw and in my mouth, and that afternoon the cranial-sacral woman does more things, not rubbing as I'd expected ("massage"), but pressure, as if my head were a jar and she places her hands just so, in particular places, as it to remove a stuck lid—firm, gentle pressure. At one point, I feel like I'm being milked, a sort of inner squirting, not at all unpleasant, and she says yes, it's the sacral fluid. She's opening the channels, letting the fluids flow. Within hours, something feels distinctly different. As if the water is slowly draining out of my ear at last, and by morning I can hear again, in both ears, perfectly. I can hear where voices and sounds are coming from, hear people talking no matter what side of me they're on. Thank the goddess. Thank you, Auntie!

But within a month, the deafness is back. I phone my two alternative caregivers and again, the coincidence of getting appointments with two very busy people on the same day, and again, within a few hours, I can feel a shift, and my hearing comes back.

Then it goes again, a month later, but this time, even two visits to the alternative doctors doesn't bring the hearing back.

So I go back—no, I storm back—to the ENT, the ear nose throat doctor—and this time I'm mad. I don't want to be rude, don't want to say "you, you told me" but I think it. Instead, I tell her that although I've been told this ear thing has no known cause and can't be cured yet here I've had it come back not once but twice. Something is still shifting so surely there's still hope for my ear and what is she going to do about it now? I finish with a flourish. There has *got* to be an answer.

She looks at me and says, “How do you know your hearing came back?”

I must have heard her wrong.

She repeats it. “How do you know your hearing came back?”

I answer lamely, impossibly, “Because I could hear.” It’s almost a question.

She’s brisk, efficient, doctor-like. I hate her. “Until we’ve actually tested you, we won’t be able to confirm that.”

“But you *did* test it!” I say, excited. I have her now. “Before, when it was bad.”

“We’d have to test it after it came back, when you thought you could hear again.”

But the reason I’m here is because—though it came back twice, and of that I’m sure, though shaken—it’s gone again. It can’t be tested now. And I stumble out, stunned.

Now what?

Slowly, I regather myself and eventually I’m furious—how dare she disbelieve me?—but I’m dangerously at the end of all my options. What now?

I become an expert on alternatives. I find strange and unheard-of-before medicines and treatments and doctors that make my partner and my father roll their eyes. My mother only looks worried. “Do what you have to, dear,” she says, and I cling to that.

It turns out everyone’s a doctor. Everyone has something to suggest. Perhaps it’s to do with your neck, one says, so you find a guy called a Grostic chiropractor who deals exclusively in necks. He is kind, fastidious, a draftsman in detail, which is good considering it’s my neck he’s fiddling with. He clears his patient list, he makes others wait while he X-rays, says that if it's pressure on a nerve, time is of the essence, and treats me so gently that as I lie on his odd-shaped couch waiting for him to begin, he tells me he's already done. It's all in the angle of the pillow he has adjusted several times under my head. I go back three times and though my neck now feels twelve inches long and I'm sure I carry myself as tall and erect as a dancer, my hearing has not returned.

I'm learning a new language. Someone says "TMJ, temporomandibular joint," something to do with jaws, and I go to a dentist who's a jaw specialist, all the way to Nanaimo because everyone there raves about him. He too is kind, makes my treatment a priority, "Though," he says, "I've never heard of TMJ related to hearing loss." He takes X-rays and when I tell him my lengthening story, he says sadly that if he were practising now in a clinic, as he once did in the United States, there'd be a whole team under one roof to consult with—naturopath and chiropractor and cranial massage and ENT and dentist, all of them talking to each other.

But my hearing doesn't come back.

The next time I go for another check-up with the ENT, it's yet another doctor. I like this, the fact that I've now consulted three or four. He is sympathetic. When I tell him about my hearing coming back twice with cranial-sacral massage, he doesn't say, "How do you know?" He says, "We try to be open to these things." This is a good sign. I'll take what I can get. He orders another test, this one to test the nerve in my left ear.

But halfway through, the tester stops and practically rips the cords connected to my headphones out of the console.

"You're wasting my time!" she snaps. "There's nothing there to test!"

I know this means "no nerve." I know that even the naturopaths say nerve does not regenerate. I leave in tears.

Life changes when you can't hear out of one ear. For one thing, as the ENT warned, you have no sense of direction. This was entirely unexpected. And the realizations—acceptances, I guess you'd say—didn't come all at once. They came in pieces, like small steps, like a diver going down or coming up slowly, in stages so she won't get sick. I noticed when my hearing first went that I wasn't very good at telling which tree birds were singing from, didn't even think about it much until one night when John, my partner, was in the bath. He called me in to chase out the wasp that was bumping loudly around the steamy little room. And I couldn't find it. I could hear it, buzzing loudly, but everywhere I looked, to the right, to the right, more to the right until I was virtually turning in circles—he wasn't. I was lost in my own bathroom.

"I guess that won't work," John said quietly. And I had the sickening realization that since only my right ear was working, everything—all sound—now came from there. I felt ill. Later I'd get the story clearer, that in the same way that two eyes give us depth perception, two ears—by the tiny differences in the speed with which sound arrives—give us directional perception. The other advantage of two ears—who knew?—is for depth. In a room full of other noises, a party for instance, one ear hears the background noise while the other screens it out, focuses in on the person you're talking to—both ears working. But if you have only one ear, it must do all the work and, like any job, it can't handle it as well as two. So at a party or a restaurant, all sound—every voice at the next table, every clanking fork, every tune blasting from the speakers, every word from your best friend—comes in at exactly the same volume. To one side.

I was a teacher at the time, and at school they had to change my classroom. That exhaust fan I'd never even been aware of before, was suddenly so noisy that I couldn't hear my students over it. Not to mention that instead of having what I'd always enjoyed as comfortable semi-conversations as students called out responses to my questions, I now had to ask them to not only put their hands up if they wanted to say something, but to wave them around to get my attention, or else I'd have no idea who was speaking, or from where.

I went public. I made a small speech in each of my classes about what had happened, surprised to find it mildly shameful. I fought the shame, telling students they had to raise their hands from now on, and that if they approached me from the left, I wasn't being rude or ignoring them if I didn't respond; I simply hadn't heard. I asked them to approach me only from the right, speak to me on my right. If there was any background talk, I heard nothing but chatter—a small, very small, bonus of having yet another reason to ask for silence in the class and concentration on whoever was talking.

I also told my colleagues at work. They only nodded, looking confused, as if I'd said I was taking a brief, inexplicable holiday. People kept forgetting, talking to me from the left. "Which ear is it?" friends asked over and over. One joked about staying on my "right" side.

It was exhausting. I couldn't understand my sudden, terrible fatigue until a friend I'd known for nine years revealed that she too was deaf in one ear, had been since childhood, and that deaf or hard-of-hearing people have to work much harder wherever there is sound. People forgot I was deaf—deafness is an invisible disability—and then thought I was rude, ignoring them, thought I was stupid for missing what they'd said. And I *felt* stupid, all those terrible gaps when everyone else laughed and I didn't get it, hadn't heard it.

I had to watch lips and faces much more closely, had more trouble hearing when a face was turned away, or in darkness. I played with that word, "disability." Other people have disabilities. I can be kind to them, understanding, and walk away only a tiny bit smug that it was them, not me. Only this time it *was* me. There was no more walking away.

~

Slowly, I got better at being deaf. I automatically slipped onto people's left sides with my good ear toward them, though often, I'm sure they didn't notice. I got so used to it that I'm now nervous when I see characters on TV or in movies talking on someone's left side. I learned to always sit at the far corner of any table, with my "good" ear to the group. I appreciated family and friends who soon learned to wait for me to pick my chair first. I learned to avoid parties—another word for cacophony. I also did my best to avoid dinner parties—more clashing of cutlery, loud as cymbals—especially in restaurants.

Restaurants were their own torture. John and I love good food, as do many of our friends. Eating out, trying different foods and different restaurants had always been a special pleasure. Now slowly we began to ask only one other couple at a time to join us, so I could hear. I read enviously about a San Francisco restaurant reviewer who carried a sound level tester and gave volume reports as a part of the quality of any restaurant.

And I got better at coping. At night if the neighbours were noisy outside, I had only to turn my "good" ear to the pillow and all was silent again—a built-in ear plug. Three years after my hearing went, I took a short course in the same room where I'd been teaching when I lost my hearing. It wasn't until the course was over that I realized I'd heard everything fine, and the fan—that same fan—was now only a minor irritation.

I got better at explaining, too. At first I'd been angry: stupid ear, only good for hanging an earring on. But now I referred to my non-hearing ear as the Silent one, felt almost love for it. And nurtured, deep down, the thought that somehow my hearing was still there, regardless of the doctors and the tests. It was still there, somewhere, just unable at this time, or unwilling, to come forward. It was merely resting.

I didn't tell people that. They would have said, or thought, I was just fooling myself, not able to accept reality, like Monty Python insisting his dead parrot was "merely sleeping." But in myself, I nurtured the small certainty that my tiny hearing self was merely waiting. For what, I didn't yet know. I would be patient. I would sink down, into the deep of myself, and wait. And listen.

The Erotics of Cutting Grass

or My Secret Love Affair with a Husqvarna

Luckily, the sound of birds, and sheep, and once in a while a wild wind, still came through in my one good ear. I was especially grateful for this when John and I, thinking ahead to our retirements, bought acreage on Pender Island where we'd first met. The island was called Pender by the Europeans who began permanent settlement there in the 1870s, and St̓éyəs (pronounced SDayes) by the Saanich peoples who've lived and hunted here for over seven thousand years. Our new place sat in a valley that ran east–west so there was sun all day and a long, peaceful vista that included glimpses of a distant neighbour's sheep. And grass. Lots of grass. Acres of it.

The purchase price included a small Husqvarna grass cutter, the kind you ride, and although John was once a heavy-equipment operator, I took on the grass-cutting job. We agreed to leave parts of the property's grass to grow as hay for our neighbour's sheep, but it was a fire hazard to have fields of tall grass too close to the house and out-buildings, so much of it had to be cut, and often.

It was all new to me—I was never attracted to even use a lawnmower. But once I'd tried the Husqvarna, it was fun. "Husky" John called it, which made it sound like a friendly dog, not a mechanical beast.

Learning how to start a Husky involves a certain ritual: check gas levels, set depth of cut, put on yellow earmuffs, pull this, push that, keep my feet here not there, turn key in the ignition and—all going well and if I've done it right—I hear the satisfyingly deep roar of the engine catching. Then I bump along, glancing back once in a while to see the land behind me reappear from under a high grassy carpet, now laid out as smooth as a tightly pulled sheet over the bed of earth.

Over time, I began to understand why my brother-in-law, a Prairie farmer, had always spoken so happily (in his own tough-farmer way, of course) about his hours and days on the tractor and even better, the reaper, on the farm. Like him, I had begun to notice bumps and hillocks of land that I'd never taken note of with mere eyes. On the Husky, I felt the earth with my entire body—where the too-steep slopes were, the rocks and mud, and how close I could get before my machine came to an abrupt halt and I had to stop and pull out the little metal thingy at the back so I could disengage the gears and heave, with all my strength, to get the machine on solid ground again. And carry on, triumphant.

I got to positively look forward to cutting grass. There was the ritual of the starting, but also of the clothes. What worked best for me was a red peaked cap I bought especially to keep sun off my face but not get in the way of the earmuffs. Plus my grubbiest blue jeans, an old fleece jacket on the cool days (thank you to my favourite second-hand store), gardening gloves, and a pruner in my pocket for the ever-encroaching blackberry bushes.

It reminded me a bit of construction. One of the things I'd most loved about building was the physicality of it. Being outdoors in every weather, acutely aware of each move my body made in case of accidents or falling, the smell of fresh-cut lumber and now, in the case of the Husky, of gas and fresh-cut grass. I'd also loved the intensity of construction, the rhythms of it, seeing the product of my labours instantly before me—or now in the case of grass, behind me.

But there was more. In talking about farming, my brother-in-law had once used the phrase "learning the land." At the time it had made no sense at all, but after a few years of cutting my own acres of grass—every small rise and dip, every hillock and flat, rounding every corner and knowing which tricky bits were coming up, getting as close as possible to the wire cages that protected our trees from deer without knocking the cages down—over time I came to know this land too, physically. Came to know where I should brace myself, how I should lean, how far away to stay from the edges of ponds and drainage ditches. It was like learning a lover's body.

I know that sounds a bit extreme and the first time I wrote it, I promptly erased it. But I had to put it back because yes, it's been that kind of intimacy, that kind of love, a physical kind of love.

I even get jealous. If John makes a move toward the Husky, I will loudly proclaim sudden plans to cut the grass myself, thank you!

Body to body. Thanks to my secret love affair with the Husky, I've come to know our small piece of this beautiful earth intimately. I love the feeling of being here with the warmth of sun on my face, the smell of fresh-cut grass and even, when I refill the tank, the whiff of gas, all the while companioned by huge evergreens waving blessings from the hills around. It's a happy marriage.

A Colonial in France

or How Not to Spill the Wine

One of the most "alive" places I've ever discovered, as Emily Carr would say, was France. Perhaps because I was raised from the age of ten in Montreal, Quebec, and learned to love the French language, or perhaps because my father was British with nothing but British scorn for all things French and, at the time, whatever my father disliked, automatically earned credit in my eyes. Whatever the reason, and with the added bonus that our son now lives there, my husband, John, and I have managed to visit France almost every Christmas for the past several years, to visit our family in Strasbourg.

On one of those early visits, within an hour of arriving I spilt a large glass of red wine on the new white carpet, an accident my son and daughter-in-law kindly blamed on jet lag, but the spill was an awkwardness that haunted me for the entire trip. There is so much beauty and grace in France, and whereas on previous visits I seem to have floated over it tourist-like, on this trip I stumbled through the thick of it, as if after a trance-inducing twenty-hour journey I had suddenly woken up—really woken up—into a world I'd never grasped before that was half magic, where among other miracles everyone spoke perfect French, even the children, and I was too dazzled to notice minor details like where I laid my wine.

For example, on the first day after the wine-spilling episode we went for lunch to a small local restaurant.

"Nothing fancy," Alina, my daughter-in-law, said.

I ordered linguini and with the first bite, no, before that—with the bread casually laid before us, with the smell of the sauce—was thrilled by one of the best pasta dishes I've ever eaten; cooked *al dente* with a creamy zest of lemon sauce highlighted with smoked salmon, washed down with a house wine better than the fine wine we'd toasted with before leaving Canada.

"To die for!" I exclaimed.

"Welcome to France!" Alina said, laughing.

It was as if I'd never seen—or tasted—France before. I would definitely taste it again!

The Bread:

In this country, bread hardly belongs under the category of food, or else it belongs at the head of the list. French breads in their many forms are an art, a grace, a manna. French men and women travel far out of their way early each morning to pick up the perfect bread, for it must be bought fresh at the right *patisserie*: long, slim loaves of *baguettes,* the shorter, flatter *banettes,* sweet and ever-so-slightly crunchy *croissants* or loaf-like dark ryes with mixed grains.

I knew French people never ate their bread with butter but one night out for supper with John, I had a craving. Very politely, I asked the *garçon* for *un peu de beurre*. The young man looked alarmed.

"*Pour quoi?*" Why?

"For the bread," I explained, sheepish but determined.

"The bread?" He was clearly puzzled.

John kicked me under the table.

"*Oui*. It's a Canadian thing—*un chose canadien*?" Ignorant colonialism was my last-ditch defence.

At that moment an older waitress swept in, said a few words under her breath and minutes later the boy returned bearing a slab of delicious French unsalted butter, eyes lowered as if not to acknowledge the travesty he was about to perform. Butter was promptly followed by a set of salt and pepper shakers, something I'd never seen before on a French table. I half expected a delivery of ketchup. For the rest of the evening, the boy refused to catch my eye. Clearly, I was *une scandale*.

"You North American, you," John smirked.

And it turned out that's exactly what I was, though I only understood it when, after I came home, I learned about a theory of international "Cultural Dimensions" developed by a Dutch man named Geert Hofstede, in which he has measured and compared five key aspects of various world cultures. One of these—the Uncertainty Avoidance aspect—indicates how a culture deals with ambiguity. At a level of 86 out of 100, France, it turns out, has one of the highest scores of any culture on Uncertainty Avoidance. In other words, rules are important. In France, butter is not to be eaten with bread.

The Commerce:

In Strasbourg, all stores close for lunch from noon to 2 p.m. How un-North American to lose the opportunity to "sell stuff" to browsing workers on their lunch breaks! But on this trip, when I took a second look, workers weren't browsing at all; they were eating—usually for the entire two hours. One newspaper reported that when a restaurant owner set a new policy that waiters must present the bill after a mere one and a half hours instead of whenever the eaters—perhaps hours later—decided to leave, the waiters rebelled in horror. Food cannot be rushed.

Maybe this has something to do with order and how things are supposed to be done, but there's another side to it. During the 12 to 2 p.m. lunch break, restaurants are open but they close again at two *précisément*. In fact, as I would later learn, once the front curtains or shutters are lowered at about 1:40, new customers are not welcome while staff finish up in the kitchen. But one day, after spending the morning in the park with our granddaughter and not knowing (yet) the two o'clock rule, we arrived at a nearby restaurant at 2:10. The front blinds were down which I thought merely a response to the bright sun. There was a strange *frisson* of hesitation when we entered, then my six-year-old granddaughter recognized the waiter from previous visits, said something to him (she is one of those amazing children speaking perfect French in France) and he seated us. Later, my son, far wiser than I in things French, was astonished they served us at all.

"We would never have had the nerve to try that," he said.

Other times we weren't so lucky. On a side-trip to Dijon I went into a shoe store to buy a pair of the brand of shoes I love. They're made in France, so instead of paying the imported price at home I figured to get a bargain. The clerk greeted me. I picked two styles and asked for my size. The woman took the shoes from my hand, leaned close and whispered kindly, "Would you mind coming back later?"

It was noon, and not even a sale could stand in the way of lunch.

The Manners:

After lunch, when I came back for the shoes, the clerk asked my size. When I said "forty-three," her eyes widened in disbelief.

"Our largest size is forty-one, *madame,*" she said, and as I turned to leave, big-foot Canadian, she made a sound almost of laughter.

Usually, manners are not an option in France. Children as young as four will extend a hand to shake when introduced, greeting you politely with *Bonjour, madame,* before running off to play. Even though I found the formality a little theatrical, I always tried to follow suit—though some of my best-intentioned behaviours, like the shoe incident, seemed to strain the bonds of French decorum. When I'd walked into the shoe store, I'd been very conscious to reply to the clerk's, *Bonjour, madame,* with my own, *Bonjour*.

I'd learned this the hard way. On a trip to Chartres Cathedral when we were late to the train station and didn't know the right track number, I'd rushed to the Information booth and urgently asked the agent, perhaps a tad forcefully, "What platform for the train to Chartres!" We were late, after all.

The man frowned, raised his chin, turned his upper body the tiniest bit away and said deliberately, slowly, *Bonjour, madame.*

This is how it's done in France: a certain formality, the rules of *politesse* demanding that every interaction begin with acknowledgement, no matter what time it was. I got it.

Bonjour, monsieur, I'd replied, looking the agent straight in the eye. "Which platform for the train to Chartres?" And he promptly told me what I needed to know.

This reflects another of Hofstede's measures of culture, the Power Distance index that measures how people accept differences in power relations and the proper ways to conduct oneself with others. A high score implies acceptance of more formal, hierarchical relations. The Canadian score of 39 is low, indicating, Hofstede suggests, generally "consultative or democratic" power relations. France has a high Power Distance Index of 68 which helps explain why, whenever I made sudden North-American-like exclamations, or became unduly excited and spoke a little loudly as I'm prone to do, people usually responded with a subtle expression of almost-pain and the barest pulling away. I began to call it "The Look" and I regularly felt it in first interactions, like when I asked the woman in the Strasbourg tourist bureau for suggestions of cities we might like to visit nearby and she gave me The Look.

"This is the *Strasbourg* tourist office!" she repeated, as if I was distinctly doltish not to have noticed. And though she'd lived in the area for years, she couldn't/wouldn't make a single suggestion for anything outside her official boundaries.

But there was bending. After a quick trip to the English language bookstore to check the travel section and narrow our choices, John and I went directly to the railway office and asked the ticket agent whether he would recommend Dijon or Besançon for our tourist visit. At first he protested; recommending tourist destinations was not his job, his job was only to get us there.... However, with some gentle pressing he looked over his shoulder as if about to commit an act barely legal.

"Besançon?" he said in a near-whisper. "Who'd want to go to Besançon?"

We bought two tickets for Dijon.

The Food:

Within hours of touching down in France, as John and I transferred trains at lunch hour for the last leg of the trip, we'd each bought a sandwich on the train platform. Where I come from, station-platform fare is reliably minimalist in quality, but this sandwich was generous slices of perfectly cooked chicken, moist with a sweet mustard sauce and sun-dried tomatoes in a luxurious bun with a crisp crust—bread I would have happily eaten by itself any day without the filling, for its texture and sweetness alone.

The French assumption of quality and freshness in their food—any food—reminded me of a time years before when we'd rented an apartment in Paris. That night I'd felt like salad for supper and headed for the local *marché*. When I laid the last head of lettuce on the checkout counter, the grocer took one look at the slightly wilted outer leaves and whipped it out of sight.

"I'd like to buy that," I said.

Non, madame.

And he explained, very politely, that this lettuce was not completely fresh and therefore could not be sold. The offending vegetable looked as good as anything I'd ever bought in a market at home so I explained I was willing to put up with a little age, I'd freshen it with cold water, throw away the outer leaves.... But the man was adamant. He wouldn't—couldn't—sell such an undesirable vegetable. Later, when I watched French women carefully inspecting produce at the ubiquitous market stalls full of fresh local produce, I understood. In France, you don't buy a week's supply of groceries in advance, none of this stuffing whatever comes first to hand into a plastic bag to eat a week later, *non! La fraîcheur*, as I had now learned, is paramount.

The Men:
As a sixty-plus-year-old heterosexual woman, I'd long become used to being invisible on the street. By age forty, certainly by fifty, there was actually ease in not having to be aware of men's eyes in public even though my own eyes hadn't stopped looking. In fact, safe inside my cloak of invisibility, they've broadened their range. I can now look at an attractive man of any age, and appreciate. I also look at attractive women and do the same without an ounce of the uncomfortable comparison that's hard to avoid when you're a younger woman under pressure to be "beautiful."

In general, I thought I didn't care anymore what people thought about my body. But in France, I now noticed, men continue to look at women—even sixty-year-old ones. At breakfast one day in the hotel I became aware of a fortyish, attractive-looking man sitting with his back to me, he with his partner, me with mine. He got up so many times for small items that I suddenly realized—in the way that women know—he was "checking me out." I'd felt it before but not so clearly; French men have a way of looking that is appreciative rather than leering. It was lovely.

The Architecture:

Perhaps because I used to be a builder, one of the great beauties of France for me is its architecture and the age of so many of its buildings, particularly its cathedrals. In a country where high-rise buildings are rare, Gothic cathedrals soar above the mostly four- and five-storey stone and wood buildings around them. It's hard to imagine the powerful impression such magnificent structures must have created in the twelfth and thirteenth centuries when they were built, reaching toward a Heaven that was utterly real to each citizen.

Inside, the cathedrals are even more impressive. I spent hours wandering, in awe of the stone-carved details of columns, pillars, arches and statues, elaborate stained glass windows half-lost in high shadow, the smell of incense and flicker of candles. Coming from a country where speed is of the essence in building, where everything is square corners and multiples of four-by-eight-foot sheets of plywood, I was humbled that generations of men (all men?) had been proud to labour on the curves and arches of a single structure for their entire lives.

I also knew that the architects—many of them the master masons on the job and especially as they made the transition from heavy Norman-style churches like Mont St. Michel to the high grace and light-filled interiors of Gothic churches like Chartres—were figuring it all out on the fly as they built, solving new problems of height and lightness. And praying as they built, that they had it right.

The Protestant churches I visited, though grand by North American standards, were far more modest. I spent time there too, the plain walls and pale windows like a refreshing drink of clear water after a complex wine.

La Langue

I was warned before my first visit that the French take great pride in their national identity but particularly in their language. The Oxford English Dictionary tells us the word "chauvinism" is of French origin, so I was grateful that people seemed tolerant of my French. They waited, more or less patiently, while I found the right word, right expression, right tense. In return, I did my best to introduce the rolling French "r" and a more precise pronunciation to my Quebec-inflected accent. But I was surprised—in a country known for its fierce protection of the "correct" use of its language, and with an entire institution (L'Académie française) dedicated to its purity—to find jarring English phrases frequently thrown into the public mix: "The Sweet Life" read the billboard in front of an apartment under construction; "Just T" said a teabag tag. In a sea of smoothly rolling French vowels, these English interjections always sounded awkward. Who wouldn't rather go to a "Palais de Nourriture," than—as I saw it described in the only mall in town—a "Food Court."

Later, back in Canada on a visit to Quebec City, I noticed another difference: in France I'd been aware of moving my jaw, my lips and mouth far more vigorously when speaking French, than English. But Quebec French went even further—something about the nasal intonation, the slur of tightly clipped vowels. If speaking French was a physical workout, France's French was a brisk walk but Quebec French was a full-on run!

What I missed:

Face cloths, bathtubs.

What I loved:

The varieties of wine, the soft white *chèvre* and whipped cheeses. The bread, the pride in food in general. The language. Cathedrals. A slower pace.

Would I go back? I can hardly wait. Perhaps next time I shall be more graceful, better at balancing my wine, and my expectations.

Seeking Home

Honouring "Why?"

> It is not words that guide me…
> It is the stillness before any name
> is given and the stillness just after.
> Peter Levitt, "Pale Shadow"

Why did I sign up for a course on Buddhism, anyway? In the 1970s, Buddhism was an unfamiliar and therefore slightly suspicious practice, verging on cult.

"Just curious," I told my friends. All I knew was that a lot of people in South-East Asia and increasing numbers of North Americans were doing this thing they called meditating, just sitting still with their eyes closed. It looked easy. I'd seen the pictures. What I didn't talk about was that, in spite of having a life full of friends and career and a loving partner, I had become aware of a growing low-key sense of unease and unsettledness. Just sitting still sounded pretty safe. What could go wrong?

So I signed up for the course, "Introduction to Buddhism," at our local community centre because the centre was convenient, and because—if my friends were right and the teacher or other students were all wackos—I could easily duck out.

There was another reason, one I only admitted even to myself much later. It was hope, I think—hope for a belief system I could trust in, lean on, one that was less eager to condemn and remodel me than the patriarchal Christianity I'd been raised in.

As a child I'd wholeheartedly embraced the rituals and language and stories of Baptist, then United Churches. By age eight, I'd announced my plan to be a missionary when I grew up. By age twelve, I was teaching Sunday school and singing in the adult church choir. However, I figured if I was going to save people, I should first clear up a few questions, like, if God is love, why do people go to war and kill each other in His name? I'd even read that Nazi belt buckles in WWII proclaimed, "God is With Us" (*Gott mit Uns*). But wasn't the American motto almost identical: "In God we Trust"? How could God be on both sides at once? How could a man walk on water? And as the years went along, why was God always referred to as "He"? Didn't Adam eat the apple right along with Eve? Etcetera.

The answers to my questions were uniformly vague and unsatisfying along the lines of "Just have Faith."

"What's Faith?" I'd ask and get another non-answer. The more I asked, the more my enthusiasm waned until by age thirty I'd rejected the church entirely and was groping for my own spiritual practice, mostly through a reverence for nature. I spent a lot of time listening to the whisper of trees and birds and water, appreciating their beauty, grateful there were no actual words, no one to talk to or argue with or ask questions of, no one telling me what to do or that my flesh was evil. Still, by then I was a carpenter and my solitary spiritual practice felt lonely, like trying to build a house without a hammer.

~

At the first class on Buddhism, eight of us sat in a stiff semi-circle as the teacher told us that in the Buddhist tradition ("We don't call it a religion," he said), we focus first on our own pain and suffering because, as he said, "How can you love other people if you don't first love yourself?"

My instant thought was, "How un-Christian!" I'd always thought you were supposed to love *others* first and yourself last, especially if you were a woman. My second thought, as I fought back sudden tears, was that it made perfect sense. Of *course* you can't love others if you don't first love yourself. I didn't know why I was crying, unless it was the feeling that someone had just offered me what might prove to be a tool.

Then came the meditating part. I hadn't realized I was nervous. The teacher said that to meditate we should sit comfortably, eyes closed, and concentrate on each breath as it came into and went out of our bodies.

That was it?

"Although sometimes," he continued, "you can also walk or lie down when you meditate."

It sounded far too simple but I did as I was told. There was a rustling as we all got comfortable, then I closed my eyes. Instantly I needed to blow my nose. I mean, *desperately* needed to blow my nose. I was about to disgrace myself with nasal runoff. I mentally smacked myself for not blowing it before we started and wondered if it would be okay to pull out a Kleenex now or would that disturb people? I didn't know anyone here except the friend who'd come with me.

It made me wonder who the others were, and what were they doing right now? Snuck a peek. They looked pleasant enough even with their eyes closed—normal, even….

I was interrupted by the teacher's voice. "When your mind is distracted by thoughts," he said, "remember they're only thoughts. You don't have to do anything about them right now. Simply let them go and return to the breath."

Right. And amazingly, when I got back to focusing on my breath, I'd forgotten about my nose. Somehow the need had passed. I inhaled, exhaled, felt the coolness on my upper lip—which reminded me I'd forgotten to take meat out of the freezer for supper. I sneaked a peek at my watch. Three minutes had passed. It felt like thirty. Oops, and I was supposed to be concentrating on my breath. Hopeless! I thought. I can't do this. But that's ridiculous, I can breathe, can't I? Although lately I've been having this sinus thing....

"Just breathe," the teacher repeated quietly from across the room. So I started again, thinking to myself I was a pitiful meditator.

Later, when the teacher told us the Buddha had advised his followers to "question everything," I felt a surge of relief. I'd always done exactly that and suddenly it was okay! I decided right then that no matter how ridiculous the breathing thing, and no matter how bad I was at it, I'd give this meditation thing a try. After the course ended, a friend I'd never suspected of Buddhism invited me to "sit" and meditate with her small group, so I went. They weren't wackos—they were people like me, looking for a little peace and quiet in their lives. So I kept going. Often I wondered what—if any—difference meditation made in my life, but there was this smallest sense of greater calm, of knowing what to do now if—when—I felt overwhelmed or afraid.

With that small group, led by a teacher named Joanne Broatch, I began to attend weekly meetings they called "sittings" where we—yes, sat—and meditated, read about Buddhism and talked. I loved the discussions, and trust me, I asked lots of questions—about Buddhism itself, its perspectives on life and how to live it with grace and without suffering, all applied to our very North American existence. Following Joanne's suggestion, I also tried to meditate at home. I was grateful that she never berated us for forgetting, or for being too busy to meditate every single day. I also began to notice small changes, like I wasn't beating myself up so often over all my failings and imperfections.

"Just start again," Joanne said gently, over and over. "Start every minute fresh." I was getting the idea this was a far more forgiving kind of practice than the sternly paternalistic, shaming one I was used to. I liked it.

Slowly the people in the group became my *sangha,* my spiritual home base. I was still suspicious, reminding myself constantly it was okay to "question everything"—which I did. If meditation often felt like doing exactly nothing, at least it never felt wrong, and when it felt right it felt gut-deep right. However long I sat—for five minutes or forty-five—I came to see how I always felt calmer after, grounded in my own shameless body, more ready for whatever the world was offering, the way it was, as opposed to the way I wished it would be. I was learning a new way of paying attention—"Kind attention," Joanne called it—to my body as well as my mind. The wonder of it was that this was attention without judgement. It was like a camera lens shining on what had once been a very murky picture. Surely this wasn't bad?

It was at longer retreats of two and three weeks, sitting in longer silences, that I first experienced the stillness I now associate with meditating, the sense of being present in, and to, the extraordinary detail and wonder of everything, including the natural world around me. It's the stillness of an animal, perhaps—quiet, alert, with nothing in mind except an intense awareness of where I am at this moment. "If there had been an emergency when I was meditating," I later thought, "I would have been instant in my response, and utterly calm." I was discovering the wonder of being uncluttered by internal, endlessly distracting talk-talk-talk. One friend called meditation "not an ideology but a methodology," though trying to describe the experience of meditation to a non-meditator is a bit like trying to describe the experience of writing poetry: language keeps breaking down. "Seeing what is," I said to a friend, trying to describe the experience, "without trying to make it look like anything else, without wishing it to be different." I could also have said, "Without having to ask 'Why?'"

When I eventually confessed to my family, all strong Christian churchgoers, that I'd started a Buddhist meditation practice, they tried to not look horrified. By now it was the late 1990s and for many North Americans, meditation was still a vaguely threatening "foreign" thing—"devil worship" some might have said, though there were no deities in sight. Buddhists don't believe in a creator God, which was definitely part of the problem for my family.

~

The practice of meditation is an ancient one that seems to have originated independently in both China and India as early as 1500 BCE, though some suggest there were even earlier forms in shamanic cultures in Siberia and Africa. And it isn't just Buddhists who meditate. For centuries, some version of quiet attention to the present moment has been followed in the Hindu, Buddhist, Taoist, Jewish, Christian, Indigenous and Islamic traditions.

But it really became more familiar to North Americans in the 1960s when the use of drugs and the rise of a counterculture encouraged spiritual exploration. At the same time, world events pushed several important Eastern teachers to emigrate and begin teaching in the West. These included the Maharishi Mahesh Yogi, who initiated the school of Transcendental Meditation, TM, which I'd also briefly tried in the 1970s; Guru Maharaji; Thich Nhat Hanh; and Tenzin Gyatso, the fourteenth Dalai Lama of Tibet, plus many others.

Another turning point in the acceptance of meditation in the West was its adoption by Dr. Jon Kabat-Zinn, a Professor of Medicine (now Emeritus) at the University of Massachusetts Medical School, where he founded a Mindfulness-Based Stress Reduction Clinic in 1979, and later a Center for Mindfulness in Medicine, Health Care, and Society. Zinn's techniques and books for using mindfulness meditation for health and to relieve stress are now taught in medical centres, hospitals, corporations, prisons, professional sports and schools around the world.

~

Over time I would learn that there are lots of differences within and between the various traditions of meditation, as there are in all other spiritual traditions, but the Buddhist lineage I'd stumbled across is called Vipassana or Insight or Mindfulness meditation. It's called a "practice" because that's the essence of what you do: you practise concentration, practise being aware ("mindful") of this moment you're in now, over and over so you can get better at it, so you can apply its calm and peaceful approach to your daily goings-on.

"Why?" I asked my teachers.

"So you can clear your mind of distraction and suffering, and react to the world more wisely, more peaceably, as it is," they said.

Most days our *sangha* finished with a compassion practice—*metta,* Joanne called it—extending loving-kindness to all beings in the universe, the hated as well as the loved, the known and the unknown, all those undergoing suffering of any kind, the creatures of air, water and earth—extending loving-kindness to all beings, including ourselves.

It was this openness that most moved me—changed me.

But I had yet another question for my Buddhist teachers and this was very important; they spoke of *non-attachment,* not spending time worrying about how to acquire this or that, or what might happen in the future or what had happened in the past. Instead, they urged, simply observe what is going on in the here and now. But I'd been a political activist most of my life, particularly as one of the country's first female carpenters, speaking out and organizing for more women in blue-collar trades. So what did it mean, when I felt an anger that called for action, to simply "be present" with it? Even the Dalai Lama, head of the Tibetan Buddhist tradition, said, "It is not enough to be compassionate; we must act."

The difference, my teachers said, lies in not being attached to the outcome. I could—I did—care passionately that there be more safe shelters and homes for the homeless, less poverty, more respect for women and people of colour and LGBTQ+ people and more women in the trades. I cared about us doing less damage to this fragile planet, and I could—I did—work my butt off trying to make those goals come about.

The trick, if I were to keep these actions consistent with my Buddhist practice, would be to do this work without getting angry if—when—my actions didn't bring about the end I wanted. Or not in the way I wanted. Or not as fast as I wanted. This was—this is—both a huge relief, and a far less stressful way to pursue political action. It's also a lesson I have by no means mastered.

It's been many years since that first cautious class on Buddhism but every time I sit, focused on my breath, I wonder again at how something so simple could so profoundly change my life. Meditation has given me a tool, a metaphorical hammer at last, with which to find delight in the moment: a bright maple leaf fallen on green grass, the kindness of an old man giving up his seat on the bus for a woman with a child. On the good days and even, perhaps especially, on the rough ones, I can find a way to greater peace. Then I can go out and pursue my political and social goals with a full heart and my full attention.

Notes from the Big-Weight Side of the Gym

It's one thing to be living in the country where there are always physical jobs to do like cutting grass and gardening and cleaning ponds, but it took a bit more work when I was still mostly in the city, teaching and writing, where most of my exercise was from the neck up and the wrists down. So I took up weight training.

It started when I began work as a construction labourer and realized that those two-by-fours are a lot heavier than they look, especially when they're wet and you're expected to carry three or preferably four at a time. But once I started "working out," as they say, I liked it. I liked feeling stronger at work and in my life in general, liked being able to move around and lift easily without getting tired, liked how the numbers on the various weight machines tell you very clearly when—if—you're getting stronger. I liked how easy it is to measure your strength by which hole you fit the pin into for the next lift. So I kept it up, even after I'd finished construction.

I also knew and liked the "guy" kind of communication there. One day, a thirty-some-year-old guy caught my eye as I approached the pull-down machine beside where he was working out. "Lats" the label on my machine said. Lats are the muscles in my back, somewhere around my shoulder blades, I think. I think this because that's where the small diagram on the machine highlights the body in red.

As most often the only woman, and twice the age of anyone

else on this side of the gym where the biggest free weights were kept, I was used to the odd curious glance from young guys. The thirty-year-old watched from the corner of his eye as I stretched to reach one of the two widely spaced hand holds already hanging above me from the machine's hook. When I turned, he was handing me the single long bar we both knew is better for this machine. I nodded. Enough said.

After years in physical labour and many hours at various gyms, I knew this kind of guy talk. Neither of us said a word, but for the next few minutes as he pulled down 80 kg with each arm on his side of the machine, and I pulled 27.5 kg with each arm on mine, we worked out "together," each simply aware that the other was there. I suppressed a smile.

You might ask why I kept coming to the side of the gym where the free weights and machines went up to unimaginable weights. It wasn't because I needed access to the heaviest weights. Twenty-seven kilos was about my max, which I guess made me officially a "lightweight." But I felt at home there, surrounded by big burly guys giving the odd grunt, the unspoken assumption that we were doing serious work together (sort of), and that if we watched each other's weights we'd do no more than lift an eyebrow at the guy pressing the most kilos. He already knew we were all watching.

Why This Side of the Gym?

Maybe it's a hangover from my construction days, maybe I'd spent too long hanging out with no-fool-around guys, but I liked the inherent competitiveness of the gym, especially on the big-weight side. On a construction job, the spur had been guys needling each other. "Look at you packing four studs today! Can you do six?" In the gym, the competition was (mostly) against yourself. Last week you lifted eighteen kilos? This week, try twenty! So I continued to go to the gym.

The Senses

No matter what gym I'm in, I rarely smell sweat. It's odd when you think of it—a gym full of guys grunting and lifting heavy weights, and no sweat? Not even aftershave? There are no signs here asking for people not to wear scents, so it surprised me. I wonder if it's because the guys (and the few women) who go, are so body conscious, they shower before they turn up? Or maybe it's the extra-strong fans? Or I'm sweating too, and don't notice?

But oh, the sounds! Every gym echoes with the hollow clank of heavy weights let down too hard, too fast, and with the groans of men stretched to their delicious physical limits, so sound escapes from them like steam from an overheated engine. I know they're proud of these sounds. They're saying, without speaking, "See how hard I'm working here? How much weight I can handle? Look at me!" Big and Too-Heavy are the badges of honour here.

Me? I don't grunt or groan, haven't ever (that I was aware of) made any sound other than an occasional puff of breath on the last few pulls. I'm that much of a lady, perhaps, not making rude noises, exercising careful control even here, even now. This seems true of most of the other women too. Thin, the line we women walk.

Only once have I ever heard a woman groan in the gym. Men groan from deep in the gut—a sound I know from any man bearing a too-heavy load, or heaving the last seventy-pound pack of roofing shingles off his shoulder and up over the roof's edge. But this woman's groan came from her head and upper body, sounding positively orgasmic. It made me wonder if there are different groans for different occasions, and we women have learned only one.

Holy Ground

As I said, there isn't much talk on the big-weight side of a gym so what there is, gets listened to. Once I heard one guy say to another, "You're on holy ground here!" I didn't turn around fast enough to see if he was joking, but I'd guess, only half. The odd time I've heard a really spirited conversation, it's like being jarred by a ruffle of alarmed birds in an otherwise silent forest. Almost always it's been two women, side by side on the elliptical machines, unaware of the unspoken rule; "Sssh! We don't talk here! This is serious work!"

Cool, Cooler, Coolest

In a weight room there are mirrors everywhere. The walls are lined with them. But these mirrors are complicated. Technically speaking, they're here so you can watch your form, make sure your butt is tucked in, or out if it's a squat you're doing, head up, back straight, and so on.

Certainly, the mirrors are well used, because a lot of men watch themselves. Not casually, and rarely when they're actually lifting weight, no. Usually when they're looking in the mirrors they're sitting still, just staring—intensely—at themselves. At first I thought they must be listening to music in their earphones, absently gazing at themselves while they concentrated on the music, but "No," my son, Kevin, said. He lifts weights too. When we discussed this one day, he was adamant. "They're admiring themselves."

"You mean, comparing themselves to other men?" I ask.

"Not really. They're just checking themselves out, seeing how good they look."

Sure enough, the next time I went, I noticed several guys were indeed checking themselves out, flexing a bicep here, taking a slightly sidewise glance there, almost flirting with themselves. And I'd thought it was only we women who admired ourselves in mirrors and passing windows!

Now I know that if you're a woman and you think a guy's looking at you when you stand in front of him in the mirror, he's not. He's looking at himself. Or trying to, and wishing you'd get out of the way.

Of course, I exaggerate—a little. When guys are lifting heavy weights beside each other, they do in fact occasionally get carried away and say things to each other. I've heard, "Watch for the lagging butt!" and, "Yeah, I've got two dogs, Charlie and Benjamin. Charlie's a girl."

I'd like to know how seriously the men take all this, because there's humour in the gym too, often of the self-deprecating kind. I once overheard a guy, finishing his workout on the techno gym, say to another guy working out on the mat in front of him, "I'll try not to step on you." And the guy on the mat replied, "I wouldn't even feel it."

As a bystander, I laughed out loud. I got it: "I'm so strong, I wouldn't feel a thing!" But of course, neither man cracked a smile, though the exchange was clear. It's part of the code: don't smile, don't show emotion even when you joke. That's cool. Coolest.

When working out in pairs, women are definitely more outgoing, more outspoken than the men. I've heard other women use whole sentences with each other, like, "Don't you look good!"

Between the men, "conversation" is more often a curt nod. One nod. Only one. Says the same thing. This is where we women get the reputation for talking too much.

The Guy Nod

It complicates it a bit that I'm usually the "old woman" amid a muscle of mostly young men. I try to ignore their curious looks when I pull the pin out of the 50-kilo slot where the smallish man before me had it for his hamstring lift, and place it—hoping no one notices—in the 20-kilo slot. I console myself that it could be worse; when I started, it was in the 13.5-kilo slot. At least I'm here! Then I poke myself; I wouldn't be anywhere else, on the other side of the gym, for instance, where the lighter weights are, and the stationary bikes and treadmills where most of the women go. I like being among guys who eye themselves, push themselves, grunt. It makes it okay for me to push myself too and okay, yes, I do occasionally watch myself as I lift.

One day as I began my regular routine, I noticed two young men giving each other the eye. They'd look at me, then at each other with a subtle toss of the head and roll of the eyes as if to say, "Get that! An old broad! In our territory!" But I lifted my chin, ignored them and carried on. I knew my form, at least, was excellent—I'd had a trainer. Forty minutes later, as I left, one of them gave me the, "You're all right," subtle Guy Nod, a sort of heads up. I tried not to feel triumphant; I'm in this part of the gym not because I want to show off my strength, but so I can show that even "old" women like me, can be (sort of) pumped. We belong here too!

Saying Hello to Fear

The gym was a great way to keep my energy up when, after my official retirement from teaching, I kept writing. They say everything gets easier, the longer you stick with it, but I'm not sure that applies to writing. Any writer, no matter how experienced, can give you an angst-filled list of reasons why writing didn't happen (again) today: there were the kids. Or a special meeting. Or the first sunny day in months, or....

Rarely do we mention, "Oh yes, and I was afraid." But perhaps Fear (with a capital "F") lurks as a larger issue in *not* writing than we give it credit for.

My memoir of fifteen years as one of the first Canadian women in construction was called *Journeywoman: Swinging a Hammer in a Man's World*, and from first draft to final publication took me twenty-five years. More on that later.

Shortly after the book was published, I did a consultation with three writers working on *their* first memoirs. One was booby-trapping herself, making sure she had no time to write; another was deeply worried about what family would say; the third was troubled by the difference between her memories of a traumatic event and the notes she'd made in her journal at the time.

I recognized their struggles. I'd gone through decades of being paralyzed by these and other issues including worry about being sued, about which tense to use, even about which genre. But I would never have said I was afraid. Of what?

Muriel Rukeyser in her book, *The Life of Poetry*, said that fear "is an indication we are cut off from our own reality." I think this also applies to memoir though I didn't understand that at the time; at the time all I could think was that maybe I just didn't want to be this exposed. Maybe I should write this as fiction?

After twenty-five years, dozens of drafts and a major change of genre, when the book finally made it to the printer as non-fiction, you'd think I could at last relax, no? No. That was almost the worst; that was when I felt something close to terror over how vulnerable I'd made myself. What if I'd poured myself onto the page just to be laughed at? What if my story wasn't anyone else's story?

Then came the launch. During the same time as I was struggling with this book, I'd launched nine others so I knew about prelaunch jitters but the memoir was different. I wept for weeks, terrified. As a carpenter I'd hung off the edge of fourteen-storey concrete towers, no problem, but on the night of the launch of a mere book, my hands trembled so badly I could barely sign my name.

I couldn't understand the fear. Maybe it had something to do with the fact that my other books were poetry or biography. Biography is clearly about someone else, though the writer's presence is implicit. As for poetry, everyone knows poets make things up. And though I'd certainly felt vulnerable in writing—and reading—my poems, I'd usually written from behind the persona of someone else: Emily Carr, Georgia O'Keeffe, Glenn Gould.

So perhaps at least some of my terror now came from the fact that for the first time in twenty-five years of writing, I'd stepped out from behind all screens into the clear—emotionally naked.

~

In the end, two things were vital in helping me move through fear to finish (and publish) the book. The first was that I figured out who I was really writing it for. Of course, I'd always thought this book was for me and my friends, about me, my experiences as a woman in trades.

I knew we tradeswomen were few in number. In 1977 my research had shown the number of women in trades in British Columbia as being 2 or 3 percent of the trades workforce—about the same as it was in the rest of Canada. In 2007 when I did that research again, the number of women was the same. During that time many of us had worked hard giving speeches, lobbying, making reports and sitting on panels. There'd been new human rights laws, mentorship programs, special introductory courses, hands-on "try-a-trade" courses and support groups for women. And still, years later, very little had changed. It still hasn't. By 2025, as I write this, it's still a mere 5 percent, varying only slightly from trade to trade across the country.

~

In his novel *Roderick Hudson,* one of Henry James' characters says, "True happiness… consists in getting out of one's self; but the point is not only to get out—you must stay out; and to stay out you must have some absorbing errand."

When I realized the number of women in trades had barely budged in over thirty years in spite of all our efforts, I suddenly found my "absorbing errand;" this story of a woman in trades wasn't about me after all. It wasn't even *for* me. This story was for others: partly it was for the business owners and foremen and policy makers who wonder why there aren't more women in their trades, but mostly it was for the women themselves—for all the ones, male or female, who might be struggling to understand the unique culture of construction, or who might want to consider it as a career. To the best of my knowledge, no one had yet written a baseline portrait of this work. I wanted her or him to have a realistic sense of the ups and downs of the trade I loved.

If I had any doubts about this change of focus it was reinforced from a surprising source. When I confessed to my eighty-six-year-old mother that I was worried that the book (still in progress) might offend our family, this tiny, fragile-looking woman planted her two feet on the floor, pulled herself out of her armchair with remarkable alacrity and announced in a stern voice, "You're not writing this book for your family! You're writing this book for the world!" Case closed.

I'd come to accept that the memoir wanted to be written—had to be written—for a larger audience, but still I was afraid or, as I would have said then, unsettled. Over the years of writing draft after draft, I'd tossed out the fiction version of the story and gone on to produce a long series of non-fiction versions: a cheery version, a preachy version, a scholarly one. But none held to my basic commitment to myself that this story must be not just true to the facts, but emotionally honest. If anyone had asked, I couldn't have exactly explained what I meant by "emotionally honest" but I was certain I'd know it in my writer's gut—did know it for short passages—when I wrote it. But after twenty years of writing, none of my completed drafts were "it." It felt like I had both the brakes and the gas on at the same time. There was something holding me back.

That "something" came when I got mad. Actually, I got desperate. I'd been doing all the things I thought a writer should do. For going on two years I'd shown up at what had become "my" seat in the Vancouver Public Library every weekday at 10 a.m., writing endless drafts until two or three or four every afternoon. And I'd written shit. Why couldn't I write this damn book? Then some wiser part of me remembered a creative writing class at UBC where I'd had the problem of a fictional character "taking off" on me, and my personal terror at losing control of her. She *was* fictional, wasn't she?

My teacher, Keith Maillard, had seemed remarkably calm.

"Just keep writing," he'd said. "See where it goes. You don't have to show it to anyone." And in front of the whole class he had me do that old Gestalt therapy exercise of sitting your character in one chair, you in the other and talking to each other. I only did it for a few minutes in class (though it felt like hours) then I wept all the way home. It was a sure sign I was on to something. But what?

A few weeks later I'd gone to the movie *Jumanji,* about kids whose board game comes alive with life-threatening creatures. In the film, the children are told they must play the game through to the end and only when they do that, will it all go away. It reminded me of Anne Cameron's story *Dreamspeaker,* with its similar theme: if you don't face your fears they will terrify, even kill you, or kill some part of you.

So, sitting in the Vancouver Public Library, I used that same Gestalt therapy trick and put my Block, whatever was stopping me from writing, into the chair opposite. Then, looking just like a serious writer, dutiful scribe, I "interviewed" my Block and wrote it all down.

First I asked it, "Who or what are you?" After a few seconds it said, "My name is Fear." I wrote it down. I'd already figured out that I was afraid of having to relive some of the darker moments I'd lived in construction, but somehow this Fear was not what I'd expected.

I said, "You're big."

And it replied, "So? You would be too, bloated as hell if you'd had to hold on to as much as I have, for as long. Why the bloody hell have you waited so long?"

I was amazed. Fear as Persona was angry, though "angry" was an understatement. When I tried to tell it how hard it had been for me to write this book, Fear yelled at me in capital letters, and it talked like a construction worker.

STOP BEING SO GODDAMNED TIMID! YOU THINK IT'S GOING TO KILL YOU TO REMEMBER SOMETHING? THEY'RE ONLY THOUGHTS, FOR CHRIST'S SAKE!

So we began to talk. The conversation went like this:

Fear: Sorry I yelled. But Christ! Okay. How are we going to do this so I can finally get on with other things? What the—sorry—what the heck do you need?

Kate: Help.

F: But you're bursting to tell. What's holding you back? What are you afraid of?

K: I'm afraid I'll explode with anger, dissolve in tears, find things to regret, wish I'd done things differently…

F: There must be a way.

(Long pause while we both quiet down.)

K: What if I had something, someone to protect me?

(Another long pause.)

Even you.

(Very long pause.)

F: No one ever asked me to help them before.

Fear seemed suddenly calmer and less—well—less fearful.

From that moment, although I didn't realize it at the time, Fear became my companion rather than my foe and the book began to be written in earnest. Every time I felt stuck, every time I felt that familiar black plug of silence settling again in my throat, I called for Fear, sometimes out loud. Fear was bigger than any of them. Fear was my champion. And on I'd write, cowered behind its huge rough back.

Still, when the manuscript was finally submitted for publication two years later, I was again afraid, and on the night of the official launch, purely terrified. I wanted this book to be honest, yes, but I didn't want to be sued, or lose friends or—worse—family members. I'd heard the horror stories about memoir writers who thought they were protecting a precious someone in the text only to find, after publication, that that someone felt betrayed and never talked to them again.

Two weeks after *Journeywoman* was published, I received the first feedback from a reader, an email from a woman who had done trades and blue-collar work all her life. It was a single line that read: "At last. Someone has told our story."

A few weeks later, I got the feared email from my mother. I'd taken out of the story every family reference I could find, anything that wasn't vital. I'd softened the many tales of my father's alcoholism and in the end decided I would stand by this book even if it did come down to someone—even a family member—

never talking to me again. After all, I reminded myself over and over, this book wasn't for me. But I knew from the way my stomach lurched when I saw the subject line of my mum's email—"Your book"—that I wasn't as confident as I'd thought. I read, "I've just finished your book. It is a story of courage, fortitude and forgiveness."

Tears rolled down my face but this time they were tears of relief. If this book was okay with my mother, it was okay.

I could almost feel my friend Fear, smiling.

Le Lunch

On one of our early trips to France, our son, Kevin, suggests we all go out for lunch.

"Lunch," to most Canadians, evokes a sandwich—a nice crusty bun perhaps, soup or salad, ice cream for dessert. Very pleasant, quite filling. Total time spent, depending on conversation: one-hour.

Not *dans La Belle France.*

The restaurant Kevin chooses is in a beautiful old house set in a windy lane in a small village near Strasbourg, very near the German border. After we're seated and a napkin has been spread with care across each lap by a stern, black-clad, no-nonsense hostess, lunch begins with an hors d'oeuvre—not to be confused with the appetizer, which will come later. The hors d'oeuvre consists of a long, narrow, gleaming plate of dark slate decorated with three tiny, brightly coloured—er—arrangements, one carefully placed in front of each of us. Am I supposed to eat this?

"It's art!" my daughter-in-law, Alina, whispers in my ear, smiling at the waitress the entire time.

We've been warned by the woman in black (who I'd thought was the waitress), then again by a jolly round woman a little less formally dressed who I realize must be the *real* waitress, that the meal we can now look forward to will be a soup, a light consommé of duck, a....

But here my French fails me, and I merely nod and try to look as serious as server #1—the one in black who is now holding her head up and aside at a taut angle that suggests we may not be *quite* the kind who could be expected to appreciate the wonders to come. However....

In the initial list, I'd caught the words for "duck" and "avocado" and had tried to lower my eyelids, like hers, as if I could already imagine all these *delices*. I was trying to be worthy. But clearly I failed, because when a dark grey tray is placed first in front of me (because, perhaps, I am clearly the oldest *madame* at the table?) I forget my French manners entirely and slip into crass North American mode.

"Wow!" I say.

The server barely shudders.

But it deserves a "Wow!" The tray is a tiny work of art. At one end is an exquisite heavy silver... thing... that looks like a tiny tin can with a lid. In the centre of the tray is what might be a doll's cracker, with a dab of *quelque-chose* white and bubbly on top. The third item is a similarly bubbly tidbit, which, I surmise by its colour, is the promised avocado, topped by a wee white cap of... *je ne sais quoi*. I have no idea.

It's like having lunch in a doll's house.

Server #1 magically reappears just as my hand moves toward the green and white button, to recommend we might wish to begin with *la soupe*?

Of course. Instead of heading straight for the green and white button, I lift the lid of the silver doodad to reveal a white (now I remember she'd said *choufleur* at some point) cauliflower soup. Or was that the centre white bit and this the *consommé de canard*—duck soup? Eating in France is turning into a game of blind-woman's-bluff. Regardless, the soup, whatever it is, is delicious, though I yearn for something larger than the teensy spoon that's offered as utensil. In that tiny sip, I hardly get a decent taste, and I resist the urge to tip the silver thimble, bottoms up. On to the bubbly green dot in the middle, which is likewise delicious—a tickle of avocado—and the white bubble, which turns out to have the merest *soupçon* of shrimp.

By the time the appetizer arrives, I'm feeling in the swing, practically French. Coming from the west coast of Canada, a place rich in seafood, I've been looking forward to trying French scallops, and when they arrive, the well-browned tops and bottoms (what *is* that elusive flavour?) are excellent. But the thin spread in the centre of the plate—clearly the high point of the presentation—tastes, well, not great. Still, under the watchful eyes of the two *mesdames* serving us, I try to look as if it's all delicious and am grateful for the tiny specs, mere memories of broccoli, dabbed discreetly on the side.

Now comes the *plat,* the main course. We've visited France enough by now that I've had my fill of the heavily fatted meats and roasts the French seem to favour, including that French delight, *foie gras*—a beautiful expression that loses something in its flat English delivery, "fatty liver." So today I've ordered the vegetarian *plat,* though I'm not quite sure what a *64° oeuf* is. Still, egg and spinach salad sounded like the right, light kind of lunch.

A 64° egg, I soon discover, is an egg poached so slowly (at 64°) that the yolk and white take on a soft, yet firm texture that's almost like whipped cream, only better. The egg lies on a bed of spinach so beautifully arranged that I have to stop and admire the art of it before picking up my fork, feeling a bit like a Canadian barbarian invading the temple of good taste. But as I take the first bite, oh, now I understand French cuisine! The spinach is familiar, yes, and the egg of course, but what spinach is this! What an egg! A texture—no—a flavour that's a tiny bit tart, a tiny bit sweet, all floating like the lightest sauce over my tongue. And the yoke! It hangs like sunshine for a moment, then slides down my throat to a golden sunset in an evanescence of spinach. Who knew? Who could have imagined, let alone created, such a dish?

And all that even before dessert. The waitress says something about "*toutes sortes de chocolat*" and I understand, "*chocolat*" perfectly. Indeed, it's delicious: chocolate mousse, chocolate cream and of course, chocolate ice cream, all served on a single tray in small, perfect mouthfuls. (Small, of course. I'm beginning to understand why French people, as a rule, are not fat.)

And the wine? "I've never had a *Graves* I didn't like," Kevin had said as he ordered, going on to explain that although it's from a vineyard just outside Bordeaux province, it can't be called a Bordeaux because technically, it's outside the boundary. Of course. Regardless of its heritage, this *Graves,* too, is all those things people say about wines that sound a bit mysterious until you sip *this* wine and suddenly "full" and "complex" and "whole" are the only way to describe it really—whatever "it" is.

We finish with coffees made the way the French mysteriously make their coffee so that the flavour and look (*un peu de crème*) is only lightly of coffee, more like meringue, or the most perfect chestnut at the exact moment you crave chestnut. French coffee has none of the crude jerkiness we North Americans know as the caffeine hit. No, in France it's a lift, ever so slight, so that when the bill settles on the table I hardly notice all those numbers as we all drift out, wondering how we've lived this long without the sensory lift of French cuisine like this. But now? *Mais oui!*

And the time? From sitting down to standing up, almost four hours. Of course! *Formidable!*

Seeking Home

I was born in Canada, but for a long time I've felt like an immigrant, hovering slightly above but not quite touching down on "my home and native land." It's not that I don't know or love this country; I was born in Calgary and have lived for extended periods in Alberta, Quebec, New Brunswick and British Columbia. But over the years I've become aware of a growing sense of dislocation.

When I first mentioned, during a reading at a local college, this slightly displaced feeling of being a born-here immigrant, I was surprised by the number of students who raised their hands to say, "Me too." Especially kids from the Prairies, like me. "I feel like I'm just skating over the surface of the landscape," one said. Given that so many of us may be the children of immigrants but were born in Canada, why do we hold this feeling of disconnection, as if there is nothing to anchor us?

I first became conscious of the issue of belonging when I lived in Montreal in the late 1960s. The Separatists and FLQ were increasingly agitating for Quebec's independence from the rest of Canada and I was deeply sympathetic. It was plain to a lot of us Anglos how a province of predominantly French-speaking peoples was being run by predominantly English-speaking outsiders, while the bulk of its wealth was funnelled to the same. My father was one of those outsiders, a businessman with a British accent who spoke not a word of French.

I tried to be respectful, but Francophones seemed to be able to tell Anglophones merely by our looks. I'd climb onto a bus and before I could ask for change in my best French, the driver was already speaking English.

Truthfully, I had no sense, no understanding of the politics going on all around me. I didn't own a TV and rarely read a newspaper. My boyfriend, a man I worked with, called himself a Separatist but even the odd report I'd heard of bombs left in mailboxes in Westmount (the wealthy and predominantly Anglophone part of the city) didn't hit me, didn't seem real until one morning my boyfriend bragged at work that, "We got another one yesterday!" Meaning another English-speaker had been killed by one of the mailbox bombs.

Suddenly it was shockingly real, and I was stunned at the violence of it. Yes, I had understood (I thought) French-Canadian anger. But killing people? And there was more; I suddenly became conscious that I was one of that despised stock, the *maudit anglais,* damned English.

My boyfriend had always assured me I was "different from the other English," and somehow the fact that I'd studied Quebec history and learned French in school from Grade 6 on, meant I'd naively never identified as Other, as one of those despised Anglophones. But now, facing my boyfriend's obvious glee, it was glaringly clear that regardless of what he said, I was an outsider and would always be. Quebec was not my place. Much as I loved Montreal, and the boyfriend, I did not belong.

So where *did* I belong?

~

The story of how I came to be a Canadian probably rings close to many. My maternal grandparents were among the first Irish immigrants—now referred to as settlers—granted land in south

Saskatchewan in 1905 on condition they farm it. My cousins and their kids still do. My mother moved to Calgary to go to high school and work, which is where she met my father, an English pilot imported to Alberta to teach in the British Commonwealth Air Training Program, preparing the hundreds of Allied pilots and crew needed for the Battle of Britain. In 1945, shortly after they met at a dance put on for local soldiers, my parents married, and after the war—and a toss of the Commonwealth dice that might have taken them (and me *in utero*) to Rhodesia—they settled in Canada. So I became Canadian rather than Rhodesian, or British: an accidental Canadian, like so many others.

In 1970, shortly after my insight with the FLQ bombings, I quit my job and left Montreal to go I-knew-not-where, to do I-knew-not-what. I bought a coach-seat ticket on the CPR train to Vancouver and told myself it was a vacation—sort of. I figured I'd look around, stop at whatever cities appealed to me and get a job in one of them. I actually applied for work and was called for an interview at the *Winnipeg Free Press*, but at the last minute, got back on the train instead.

The first thing that hit me, even before the train reached Vancouver, was the mountains. Of course, I'd spent the first ten years of my life in Calgary, and a weekend trip with the whole family to Banff, in the Canadian Rockies, was a regular treat. Plus, with the flatness of our view east, across prairie, I'd always loved the sight of towering grey rock and white glaciers to the west. But by now I hadn't seen real mountains for years. When I was about eighteen years old in Montreal, my girlfriends once took me to see "the mountains" north of the city. After driving for what seemed hours, I asked when we were going to get to the mountains, and they looked at me in stunned surprise.

"They're all around us!" they said. "We've been driving through them for the past hour!" But to me, with all due respect, the Laurentian Mountains were mere foothills.

In Vancouver, I stayed at the Cool Aid Hostel where everyone told me I had to see this place called Stanley Park. So on my first day, I dutifully hitchhiked downtown. I'd already been awed by glimpses of the Pacific Ocean, but as I walked up a slight incline from the parking lot toward the duck pond on my way into the park, I stopped, smitten.

I was looking up at the most formidable tree I'd ever seen in my life. I could never have imagined such majesty. Its branches stretched out wider, fuller, greener, than anything I'd seen before. This tree had power and an almost regal presence—not to mention incredible girth. I had never seen a tree that couldn't be embraced easily with one arm. For this giant, I had to take ten or fifteen steps to walk around it, my hands sliding over its complex, ticklish texture and the rich brown of its bark as it sheltered me under a vast sweep of branches. Branches? No—arms! It felt almost human, this tree. It almost spoke, whispered in a light breeze, so visceral, so powerfully rooted, present. And there were others, all around.

In that moment, I found home. I knew it with utter certainty. I would live here, near these trees and this ocean, these mountains, for the rest of my life.

~

The well-known children's educator, Maria Montessori, believed that the landscape where a child is raised is imprinted, that the child will always feel most comfortable there. Yet I, who was raised on the flatness of prairie and in the low hills of Montreal, only felt at home near ocean, under giant evergreens. At the time, I didn't worry about the contradiction. No big deal.

The salt fell into this stew in the summer of 1998, when John and I went to Europe where Kevin, our son, was studying. By now I was a ticketed journeywoman carpenter who'd built in wood and concrete, high rises and houses and bridges, and I loved the art and power of building. But European buildings were not "old" as we say in Canada, especially in western Canada, meaning they've been around for maybe fifty years. No, these were old as in five hundred years, the age of my cousin's house in England—nothing special, he thought. These were old as in two thousand-year-old cathedrals and the five thousand-year-old standing stones we saw in Avebury in southern England.

In these countries, history swells out of every carved stone and every step is part of a long, deep tradition. I especially loved all the ancient buildings with details no North American would dream of adding today, given our preoccupations with space and speed.

Everywhere, I felt new to these places, yet at the same time, a strangely intimate sense of familiarity. When people talk of roots, is this what they mean? This odd feeling in my feet, in my hands, as if these stones were alive—this feeling of physical connection to the land, through my body, through unknown ancestors? This feeling of almost-remembering?

In Freiburg in southern Germany, we hiked up the bell tower of the city's main cathedral. At the top, we stood in a small stone space where huge church bells hung from massive wooden beams. When I absently, automatically reached out to touch one, I had a sudden, unquestionable sense that I knew this beam. At first I thought it was simply because I was a carpenter and knew wood: I'd laid my hands on plenty of beams.

But it was more than that. It was a feeling of utter certainty that I had been here before. Here, where I had never lived, never even visited, where to the best of my knowledge I had no ancestry at all, was where I could say, "I belong."

It was confusing.

~

So where exactly do I belong? Where is "home"? How am I—born Canadian—to feel at home in a land so new to my ancestors, to my blood? Here, in what many call one of the best places in the world to live, I ask, "Where is here? How shall I belong?"

When I ask at my local library for help in finding out how many of us are first- and second-generation Canadian, even the omnipotent librarian can't help. An article by historian, Danile Panneton, in *The Globe and Mail* on May 15, 2021, reported that a century and a half ago, Statistics Canada wouldn't even allow Canadians to identify as ethnically Canadian for fear of creating fragmentation—not with First Nations, but with French Canadians. That's changed, but in 2021, only 32 percent of us identified as being of Canadian ethnicity. The rest name a long list of countries that includes the British Isles, France, Germany, Italy, India, Ukraine, Holland, Poland, Philippines, Russia, Norway and so on, yet no census asks, "How long has your family been here?" In a country of immigrants, shouldn't this be an important question?

~

Sometimes, for relief, I fall into the company of comedians. Canada seems to do well in this field: Wayne and Shuster, Bob and

Doug Mackenzie, Codco, *This Hour Has Twenty-Two Minutes, Double Exposure, The Dead Dog Café, Schitt's Creek*… the list goes on. Many—most—of us may be new here but humour is an anchor. When it's scary, when you're lost, what better (Canadians seem to say) than to laugh? Judging from my dour immigrant grandmother, I doubt the first settlers laughed much. They were too busy trying to survive. Interesting then, that there's a deep tradition of humour in First Nations communities. Maybe laughter is in the land itself and we settlers, some of us, have begun to catch it.

Does that mean we can stay? The feminists say, "She who laughs, lasts." Like the traditional Swiss who yodeled over mountains, maybe laughter is the Canadian way of telling our different stories across a vast land mass and the hillocks and mountains of difference?

—

There are other possibilities.

The late writer, Robert Kroetsch in his book, *The Lovely Treachery of Words*, asked, "Exactly where are we, anyway? What is this place where all of us (except native peoples) are such newcomers? What is 'home' for a Canadian?" Born and raised on an Alberta farm, Kroetsch spent much of his adult life teaching in the US, writing about being Canadian. He speaks from exile. Which made me wonder: Perhaps it's exile that can tell us more clearly who we are?

Kroetsch goes on, "How do you establish any sort of *close* relationship in a landscape… whose primary characteristic is *distance*?" And answers, "The telling of story—more literally, the literal closedness of a book—might be made to… contain space."

Certainly, immigrant Canadians have always told stories of this place, of the land: Susannah Moodie, W.O. Mitchell, Earnest Buckler, Ethel Wilson—the list is long. Painters have also struggled to paint Canada: Lawren Harris and the Group of Seven, Jack Shadbolt, Emily Carr.... Troubadours like Gordon Lightfoot and Stan Rogers have sung its landscape. And poets. A strong tradition of the Canadian long poem has emerged, as if this land is too large to hold short ones. Shane Koyczan's long poem, "We Are More" that he recited at the opening ceremony of the Olympics in Vancouver in 2010 was a huge hit—not just with Canadians. In trying to define Canada, he said, "We are an idea in the process / of being realized," and "the effort is what makes us more." That too.

Maybe my yearning for connection to the land has something to do with a yearning for stories, starting with family stories. I used to love it when my aunties talked about life on the farm—how Grandma watered her huge garden by hand with buckets carried, one at a time, from the cellar storage tank because the farm had no running water. How Grandpa kept bees that produced the honey we ate. How, when my parents got married—the daughter of an Irish Protestant to the son of an Irish Catholic—they both received a telegram saying, "Never come home again." Though luckily, both sets of parents later relented.

All his life, my father, the English immigrant, complained of how wishy-washy Canadians are and how admirable the Americans. "Look how proud they are of their heroes!" he'd say, and rhyme off a list, telling me stories of Davey Crockett and George Washington. I always thought he was hero-worshipping Americans, but only recently have I wondered if he was asking,

"Where are the Canadian stories?" and, "I want that, too." In England when it came time to study Canada, Dad told us, his teacher ran a hand over the huge pink block on the world map labelled Dominion of Canada.

"Wheat," he said. "Now, let's get on to some rousing English history." And back to the stories.

In French, the word for history, *histoire,* also means "story," and the motto of the province of Quebec is, *Je me souviens,* "I remember." My story is my history. Immigrant Canada as a nation has a very short history, a short story, but telling stories, I become increasingly convinced, is one of the keys to the sense of community we have lost, or never really had and are now searching for. The CBC Radio legend, Peter Gzowski, dubbed "Captain Canada," knew this; it's why people who for years had tuned in to the storytelling of every kind and colour of his guests, cried when his talk shows, *This Country in the Morning* and later, *Morningside,* ended.

Indigenous peoples tell us that traditionally, their stories were told over and over to succeeding generations. Stories held implicit a lesson and a collective memory that emerged from—and was embodied in—their surrounding landscape. Stories were the soul, the essence, of community. Lately, us non-Indigenous people are beginning to listen: to writers like Maria Campbell, Gregory Scofield, Richard Wagamese, Eden Robinson, Marilyn Dumont, Lee Maracle, Michelle Poirier Brown—the list is long and rapidly growing. Perhaps movements for justice like Truth and Reconciliation and Black Lives Matter are forcing all of us to pay closer attention. But what exactly are we paying attention to, and what should we do differently?

—

Perhaps because we don't know what else to do, we make a mark. This seems to be a peculiarly immigrant desire. In our eagerness to prove we're really here, we settlers have cut trees, fenced the land ("my" land), dug mines, flooded whole valleys for our power needs, built wood and concrete towers and shelters that might be cold and damp but that will last "forever." Indigenous peoples traditionally prided themselves on being invisible upon the land. They called it "respect." Is this because the land is so deeply within their being that it was unnecessary to mark their place? Is it because their right feels so inalienable, so unimaginably deep? No wonder we immigrants must carry weapons: More ploughs! More cement mixers! These are our elders. They shall rumble and rip and belch black smoky stories that all can see, that no one can deny!

But is this all we immigrants are capable of? Robert Kroetsch said we must "salvage ourselves," not by counting or measuring, "but by the lovely treachery of words," by telling each other the stories that feed our individual and collective spirit.

What kind of collective story might our immigrant story be?

—

Robin Wall Kimmerer is an Anishinaabe biologist, a member of the Citizen Potawatomi Nation. It was in her book, *Braiding Sweetgrass: Indigenous Wisdom, Scientific Knowledge and the Teachings of Plants*, that I finally found clues to this mystery I've been struggling with.

In talking about how lost she felt when she first moved from the east to the west coast of the US, Kimmerer tells the story of the beginnings of the world according to traditional Potawatomi storytellers. She compares her feelings of being unknown and unrecognized in her new, very different geography, to those of Sky woman, First Citizen, who fell from Skyworld onto a speck of land. "The Mother of the People was first an immigrant," Kimmerer writes.

When I read it, I froze. First Peoples were also immigrants? So there's hope for us late-late-comers?

Kimmerer asks the vital question, "What happens when we truly become native to a place, when we finally make a home? Where are the stories that lead the way?" And how does a nation of immigrants, "learn to live here as if we were staying?"

But just as I'm getting excited that there's hope for us settlers, she says, "Immigrants cannot by definition be Indigenous. *Indigenous* is a birthright word." Of course, she's right. How can immigrants ever be "First Peoples"? We're several thousand years too late for that. But if we weren't "first," perhaps there's another way?

I think one of the clues is in Kimmerer's suggestion that we need two eyes—one the questioning, scientific eye, and the other the respectful, honouring eye. She asks again, "Where are the stories that lead the way?"

We settlers need to find our own stories, first, by paying attention to where we are, to the land. Every morning now as I walk my puppy, I give thanks for bird song, for the shimmer of forest reflected in ocean, for the sheep calling to each other in a neighbour's field farther down the long, green valley we now call home. It is magic, this place. Or perhaps I should say, this is a place, a land, where I have learned, or at least I have begun to learn to recognize, the magic that is here.

These days I lay my stories and poems over the land, hoping that if enough of us do this, we shall indeed create "a land to light on," as poet Dionne Brand says, a place to rest, maybe even to take root. With overlapping stories told in many languages, from many traditions, each ancient in its own right, perhaps we can build our country backwards, from the ground up, can start by planting our feet on a foundation of ancient trees, vast landscape, clear water and high mountains. We might create a foundation, one stone—one beam, one precious story—on top of another. Archeology reversed, taking notes from the First Nations who've been doing it for centuries. What a unique nation such a creation might be! Let us hope we can do it well enough, with respect for each other and each other's stories, so that in time more of us will feel—not immigrant, not settler—but home. At last.

Greeting Rock and Stone

From the time I was thirty until I was forty-five, I was a construction worker: labourer, apprentice, red-seal carpenter, building contractor, and finally a teacher of construction. Later, I taught creative writing and started publishing books. Before all that, I was a receptionist, secretary, childcare worker and lumber piler, and after that, a poet and full-time writer. You might say I've had many lives. That expression really struck home a few summers ago when John and I spent two weeks travelling around the Dordogne region of southwest France, an area famous for the beauty of its white limestone Gothic castles and cathedrals.

As someone who's worked in the trades, I pay a lot of attention to the structures and buildings around me. I'm one of those weird tourists who stare, fascinated, into the ditches dug around old buildings, examining ancient foundations. I'll also stand and watch guys mix concrete on the streets of Paris—usually much to the confusion of the guys mixing concrete.

But on this trip, I'd been smitten in particular by the Gothic castles, churches and cathedrals this southern area of France is noted for. Often from a distance it was hard to tell the difference between the three, though as you got closer, the spires of churches and cathedrals were a marker. Otherwise, those two could look identical, differentiated only by the fact that the cathedral is the seat of a bishop, while a church is not. For this reason, cathedrals are often more elaborate.

I was amazed by the complexity of cathedrals' designs, their vast heights and towers, the seemingly infinite stone details including sculptures inside and out, and the extraordinary light and colour shining from hundreds of hand-crafted stained glass windows—all built hundreds of years ago. The great French sculptor August Rodin loved the play of light and shadow, "which gives rhythm to the entire structure and makes it live."

My fascination wasn't entirely new. I've long been interested in all things medieval, from that period in Europe that stretched roughly between 1100 and 1400 AD, commonly called the Middle or Dark Ages. It started with a wonderful history teacher in university, Dr. Murray Tolmie, who from Day One enlightened us on how this was *not* a time of ignorance but of enormous creativity.

So now, decades later, when John and I rented a car and drove through the small towns of the Dordogne including Sarlat and Périgieux, and yet-smaller places like Beynac-et-Cazenac, Castelnaud la Chapelle and Rocamadour, it was a wonderful shock to find that we were in the heart of the Middle Ages with cathedrals, churches and castles everywhere. "One thousand castles in this province alone," a local woman boasted, and sure enough, when I looked around, I counted eight from where I stood.

But it was the Gothic cathedrals and churches that captured me. It was overwhelming to walk through soaring corridors, ceilings hundreds of feet above, all curved and embellished in dazzling white stone, many of them over 150 feet high—that's fifteen storeys for us North Americans—with great intersecting arches, pillars and, everywhere, statues carved from huge blocks of stone. On sunny days this space was filled with dazzling light shows from stained glass windows that told Bible stories and showed masons and carpenters at work, building them. For me, it was breathtaking, although after his first few cathedrals, John lost interest. We got into the habit of him dropping me off at the door of the next cathedral then going for a coffee at one of the many sidewalk cafés, where I'd meet him later.

My interest in the construction of these amazing spaces only built with increased exposure. How did masons and carpenters and labourers—mere humans—lift, let alone carry, such vast weights up hundreds of feet without benefit of engines or hydraulics? How did they carve stone? They had no cranes or backhoes, no power tools, though later I found they'd developed rope winches and pulleys and other ingenious mechanical devices for lifting and building, all of them based on human labour.

One thing was a bit odd. Usually, when I see an interesting piece of woodwork or a wood structure, I want to touch it, run my fingers over the grain, feel the cuts, see how another carpenter crafted their joins. Though most tradespeople won't tell you, building is a seriously sensuous pleasure. It's one of the great and secret joys of construction, that moment of approaching a fresh pile of lumber each morning, feeling the heft of the first armful of two-by-fours, the crisp smell of sap.

Which meant I was a little surprised that in these French medieval cathedrals, I didn't feel a need to touch, or smell, the stones. Once in a while I'd put out a hand to feel a cool, pale wall, or trace the mason's unique mark, his (or her) signature in stone, but somehow it seemed I already knew what to expect, or at least, it was enough to look and admire. Mostly, I was in awe of how all this beauty had been powered by simple human labour, by two- and four-men teams turning winches that allowed them to lift hundreds of pounds of rock, whole generations working on a single building, every stone laid, they would have said, to the glory of God.

When cathedrals and other old buildings are allowed to decay or are renovated, the stones are re-used for building and repairs elsewhere. Which means blocks of beautiful white stone—clearly from the old cathedral—can be seen randomly in walls all over town. At one point, walking down a back street, John and I came across one of these stone blocks lying where someone was doing a renovation. It was about two feet long, sixteen inches wide and eight inches thick. When we tried to lift it, to get a sense of the weight of these things, we couldn't budge it.

Awe took another turn when we decided to treat ourselves to a luxurious final week in France with a stay in a rebuilt mansion called Domaine de Monrecour. Monrecour was originally built of stone in the 1500s by the lords of the nearby fortress of Beynac because they wanted a more comfortable place to live, as well as another agricultural estate from which to supply food for the castle-dwellers. After a series of renovations and rebuilds, it was opened as a hotel in 1998.

When we went to check it out, the clerk at the reception desk took us up a wide stone stairway to show us the room where we might stay if we decided to spend the week there.

But this wasn't just another room. It was beautiful, yes—large, especially by French standards, with windows on three sides. There was a huge, by Canadian standards, carved walnut cabinet for clothes, a small, round, carved wooden table with two padded chairs, a warm grey carpet and a four-poster bed with white pillows and bright red curtains.

But a very odd thing happened. As soon as I entered that room, as soon as I saw that bed and high ceiling, I knew with utter certainty I had lived here before, in the Valley of the Dordogne, in this building, and that when I was here, I had been extremely happy. Now my body flushed with joy. I was home.

I was stunned at my response. Could it be coincidence? Perhaps a fluke that the room reminded me of a picture I'd once seen? But no, this wasn't a thought, wasn't a mental thing I had just experienced. It was utter, visceral certainty that I had been here before and was now back. Over the next week, every time we returned from another daytime excursion, my body was suffused with the knowledge of it, had this same unquestionable delight at coming "home." There was no doubting my enormous pleasure, my sense of deep familiarity with this place.

But I'd never been here! In past years we'd often gone to Strasbourg in northeast France to see our family there, and as a young woman in 1968, I'd hitchhiked with a friend through Spain and France. But even if we'd been through this area, which I knew we had not, we'd always stayed in youth hostels. There was no way we could have afforded a hotel. And it wasn't even open to the public as a hotel until thirty years after we'd passed by this region!

So when John and I left to fetch our luggage and come back the next day, I had to deeply question what had just happened. How was it possible that a more than five-hundred-year-old space was utterly familiar? Could I have actually been here, lived here, in some form, at some long-ago time?

Over the next few days, the countryside, architecture, cathedrals, churches—somehow everything in the neighbourhood was familiar, comfortable, "right." I had that same strange response of not needing to touch anything—stone or otherwise—because I already knew it, in my body. Every time we returned from another outing to surrounding towns or—even more spectacular, to visit the prehistoric cave paintings of the area—as soon as Monrecour came into sight I felt the same deep delight and familiarity.

What was also strange was that at about this time, I found myself writing a new set of poems about working with stone—in the voice of a female stonemason of the Middle Ages. A woman mason in those times was highly unlikely, of course. The Middle Ages was utterly patriarchal. With the possible exception of noble and royal women, the abuse and rape of women was common, including metal masks for women who spoke out too much, with a mouthpiece that damaged their tongues—"scolds' bridles" they were called—and metal chastity belts to assure that no other man could "have access" while the head of the house was away. No, it was highly unlikely that men of that time would have allowed a woman the highly respected position of trained mason. Besides, she wouldn't have been, couldn't have been strong enough.... Could she? Isn't that what they used to say, still say, about us women carpenters and bricklayers and boilermakers?

But every writer knows a poem when it comes to them, and if you're wise, you don't question it. You can always throw it in the recycle bin later, and besides, this was all just a fantasy, right? So I began writing what became, by the time we returned home, a short series of poems about a girl in the Middle Ages who is abused and hides herself by cutting off her hair to pass as a boy, and then, to support her/himself, takes up an apprenticeship in masonry.

Back in Canada, I ended up in the library under a pile of books about the Middle Ages and masons and cathedrals, and found out some interesting facts. For example, one book said women *did* have a role in building cathedrals, not as masons but as mortar and plaster mixers. This was vital work, especially mortar mixing. Mortar was, and still is, the glue that holds bricks and stones together in a wall. If the mortar isn't mixed, or doesn't set properly, a wall can sag or fall. Today, the mortar that masons use is basically the same mix of sand, cement and water that was used hundreds of years ago, though in those days the mortar wasn't brought onto a job in premixed bags like it is today. It had to be made—some of it perhaps by women. I imagined them burning the local limestone, then mixing the mortar in large clay pits using wide wooden paddles and producing the exact amount of mortar, in the exact mix, called for by the master mason for each day's work.

Also in my research I found out that after stonework was done, many cathedral interiors were coated in plaster. Here too, one text said women were sometimes hired. Plaster—like the drywall "mud" used today—was spread over the finished stones to give a smooth surface on which to paint the decorations and place the hangings that were the final finish to a cathedral.

When I read about the plaster, I suddenly remembered an incident from my childhood. I was about eight years old when my parents bought their first house, and one night they invited me to come along to see how construction was going. The builders had just finished their plasterwork. This was in the 1950s, before we had the four-by-eight-foot sheets of drywall, also called wallboard or sheetrock that I would work with as a carpenter years later, to cover two-by-four stud walls. In those early days, interior walls were created not with drywall but with strips of wooden lathe nailed across the studs and covered by hand with several coats of plaster.

I don't remember exactly what happened after I went into the front hall of the new house in Calgary. Only that suddenly my dad's voice behind me was sharply asking, "What do you think you're doing?" And I realized I was standing as close as I could get, "plastered" to the new wall, my arms and hands outstretched as if to embrace it, my nose pressed to the sharp, salty, intoxicating scent of plaster.

Back at my desk in Canada, I started some cleanup work, going through old journals to pull out rough drafts of poems, planning to start my next book. Many of the pieces had been written years ago, but I couldn't get over how many were about rock and stone. There is some debate about the difference between rock and stone. I've heard people say stone is simply smaller, or rock is made up of mineral and stone, or stone is rock that has been cut and shaped. I tend to the latter.

What a coincidence, I thought as I found more and more stone and rock poems. Clearly, my interest had started long before our trip to France. I'd been writing poems about this fascinating material for years, but so absent-mindedly that I hadn't even noticed.

Speaking of coincidence, while we were visiting the family in Strasbourg later, my daughter-in-law found a reference to a woman mason who worked on the famous Strasbourg cathedral. I was thrilled, even more so when she showed me a photo of a statue of the woman, Sabina, standing at the side door of the cathedral opposite a statue of her father, who'd been the architect. When I went looking, I had trouble finding it until I stumbled across a street called *Rue des Ecrivains,* Writers' Street—and I knew I was on the right track.

The pieces kept adding up. I'd told more than one friend that although I loved being a carpenter, if I'd been given my choice of a trade instead of stumbling accidentally into construction, I would have picked stonemason. And it's a family joke that my coat pockets are always filled with stones I've found on beaches or on hikes. Stones are spread across my windowsills and on my desk. Was it possible—maybe? perhaps?—that in some former life I had been a stonemason in the Middle Ages? Maybe, perhaps, I even once worked as a mason on the Monrecour mansion, or lived there. Who could know?

When I returned to British Columbia, I dared tell a close friend about my strange experience of being "home" in a medieval mansion. She was thrilled to hear it; she'd had similar, rationally inexplicable experiences. A second friend likewise had once "remembered" something she couldn't have experienced in her current life.

In the end, I decided that while my experience isn't rare, it certainly isn't much talked about. And really, I don't need an explanation. I know I had an undeniably powerful, inexplicable experience of memory and of joy in a medieval hotel in France, and I am grateful. Perhaps the point is not to figure it out, but simply to enjoy my memories of the beauty and history of that part of France and, for the next while, the fun of imagining and writing the life of a woman mason in the Middle Ages.

Je Suis Charlie?

Wednesday, January 7, 2015

This is the day we see a much darker side of France. I'd always thought History happened only in books, but on January 7, 2015, I learned that any day can become History. Today, for example, when I'm not looking, when I'm just another tourist in Paris having had a pleasant day enjoying art galleries, a long lunch, and now an evening stroll along the Champs-Élysées with my partner, John. Yet this ordinary day roars into History as five police vans suddenly race by, sirens screaming; as we turn a corner and notice two men in military uniform leaning against an apartment door, machine guns balanced casually across their hips, alert to our passing; and as the text message comes through from our daughter-in-law in Strasbourg, saying, "There's been a shooting in Paris. Are you okay?"

My first inclination is to laugh—of course we're okay! Neither of us has ever been near "a shooting." But as we continue to walk, I notice a heightened alertness. It's in the sirens and the machine guns. It's in the voice announcing on the Metro ride to the hotel that this train will not—repeat *not*—stop at the Place de la République. And it's in the four fully armed soldiers who step onto the Metro as we step off.

In the hotel room we immediately turn on the TV but get only a French-language station I struggle to understand. The announcer is giving "hommages" to twelve people who've been killed—did he say twelve?—at *Charlie Hebdo*, a satirical comic magazine whose offices are only one kilometre from our hotel. Just that morning, as we passed a newsstand, I'd noticed their current edition, headlined, "The True Story of Baby Jesus," showing the view between the legs of a jubilant Virgin Mary giving birth, her hairy crotch barely obscured by the head of a very manly-looking baby. I'd thought of buying it for a Christian friend before deciding it would more likely offend than amuse her. Only later do I learn that *Charlie Hebdo* takes pride in offending everyone.

We find an English-language TV station where the announcer is telling us that past issues of *Charlie Hebdo* included cartoons picturing the prophet Muhammad, something forbidden by the Muslim faith. The shooters, he says, had called out to Allah.

But we're not Muslim and don't understand. How do you justify killing twelve people over a cartoon? With news of the shooting on every channel, we watch TV as intently as we haven't done since September 11, 2001, and for once I don't mind that John flicks channels: BBC, CNN, Al Jazeera, the French language channels. Perhaps someone can make sense of this?

Yes, all reports confirm, twelve have been killed—ten cartoonists in the offices of *Charlie Hebdo,* plus the two police guarding them; there had been threats before. There's irony too—one of the dead policemen was Muslim. An amateur video is played over and over, showing attackers with black hoods almost casually going back to shoot the wounded policeman on the sidewalk, then stooping to pick up something dropped before getting into their car and driving away.

How is this possible? I knew that France, like Canada where we live, has strict gun control laws. Unlike in the US, there is no "right to bear arms" in France, and to own a gun you must first acquire a hunting licence and for that, pass a psychological test. The licence must then be regularly renewed and each renewal requires the psychological test.

We know none of this as we huddle over the TV in our hotel room. For us, it's all horrific, and the French response is swift. The reason for closing the Place de la République wasn't that the shootings were there, as I'd first thought, but because hundreds of people had already gathered, less than six hours after the killings, to hold up candles and pencils and signs saying *Je suis Charlie* (I am Charlie), evoking John F. Kennedy's *Ich bin ein Berliner* (I am a Berliner) indicating they were not as alone as they might have otherwise felt during the siege of a divided Berlin in the '60s.

When we leave the hotel to go for supper, for the first time in my life I don't take my public safety for granted. Canadians haven't experienced war on our soil since the nineteenth century—though most French reports that day included as an example of recent world terrorism, the single Canadian soldier recently killed at the War Memorial in Ottawa.

Now, the violence is here, one kilometre away.

Over the next few days there's a torrent of news about the killings, including interviews with analysts and scholars, several of them Muslim. Everyone asks the same questions: Why? And how can such violence be stopped? Predicted, even? Many of the attempts to answer refer to the status of young Muslims in France—undereducated, unemployed, scorned as "immigrants," even those who were born here. No one says "racism," though it's a clear undercurrent.

And then there's more.

Thursday, January 8, 2015

A policewoman is shot by a self-proclaimed Muslim-terrorist, and the two brothers who committed the killings at *Charlie Hebdo* take a hostage at a print shop north of Paris that is now surrounded by police.

What do you do when your simple pleasures as a tourist are interrupted by History, by horror? You carry on. Today we're scheduled to return to our family in Strasbourg but first we'd planned to visit Notre-Dame Cathedral, a magnificent Gothic structure in downtown Paris dating from 1106. It's called in the tourist books, "the soul of Paris."

Which is how, on Thursday, we happen to be standing in front of Notre-Dame when there's a sudden peal of bells so loud and deep it comes through the soles of my feet, and I remember that President Hollande called for a minute of silence today—now. A ten-minute carillon from the cathedral rouses the pigeons so that along with the bells comes a torrent of birds sweeping over like a grey shawl while below—how did they gather so quickly?—the square in front of the cathedral is suddenly filled with people, all of us standing silent. A soft rain begins to fall as the bells peal on.

That few minutes of silence is reassuring in a way that surprises me. I'd thought I was tough. I'd thought I was strong. This isn't even my battle—or is it? But the fact is that right now I'm scared, and in this moment, in a "foreign" country with all these others around me paying their respects too, I feel safer.

Friday, January 9, 2015

The next day, back in Strasbourg with the family, we're glued to TV and newspapers. There's yet another hostage-taking, this time by a man and woman at a kosher market where police immediately move in. This time, four hostages are killed, five injured, and if it weren't for the quick action of one of the clerks hiding customers in the freezer, many more might have died. One of the dead hostages is a Muslim. The male terrorist is killed but the woman escapes. Later, France will acknowledge the life-saving actions of the clerk—another Muslim immigrant—by granting him French citizenship, highest honour in a country that doesn't give citizenship easily to children of non-French parents, even those born on French soil. The ironies and complexities of this issue continue. One newspaper notes how this man, now a hero, had applied for citizenship before, and been refused. And why are terrorists now attacking a Jewish market?

Then we hear that the two men who did the *Charlie Hebdo* killings had come out of the print shop shouting their wish to be martyrs, and were granted that wish instantly, shot by police. Their hostage came out after them, safe and unharmed, telling reporters how respectful the two men had been.

With every news report, the picture grows more complex. Simple categories of "good guys" and "bad guys" seem useless. Gestures of unity like the moment of silence at Notre-Dame, and *Je Suis Charlie* signs and posters urging peace, speak from every corner, spread large and loud across every newspaper, politically Right and Left. In Paris, Catholic, Orthodox, Protestant, Muslim, Hindu, Jewish and Buddhist spiritual leaders all meet, publicly link arms and head a huge march singing Beethoven's *Hymn to Joy* to affirm their commitment to the values of liberty, fraternity and equality—the French national motto.

Sunday, January 11, 2015

The fragile sense of safety I'd felt in that minute of silence at Notre-Dame is reinforced when, in Strasbourg, a city of fewer than three hundred thousand people, we walk in solidarity with forty-five thousand others. I'm not sure if we're protesting, or affirming, or simply honouring the dead, but it feels good to be in this crowd—together. In Paris, three million others march at the same time, the largest public demonstration since the liberation of Paris after WWII. The demonstration there is led by forty of the world's leaders including from Israel and Palestine, arms linked. The fact that the senior women in the line including Angela Merkel, Chancellor of Germany, and Ann Hidalgo, mayor of Paris, are air-brushed out of the picture "for reasons of modesty" when it's printed in an extreme Orthodox Jewish paper, only adds to the complexity of this story.

For the Strasbourg march, our seven-year-old granddaughter has made herself a *Je suis Charlie* sign on a page torn from one of her school notebooks. In the absence of a suitable stick in her parents' apartment, the sign is taped to a straw she now holds high above her head. In addition to the hundreds of *Je suis Charlie* signs around us, we spot others saying things like, *Je ris, donc je suis,* (I laugh, therefore I am), a take-off on the French philosopher and mathematician René Descartes, who famously declared, *Je pense, donc je suis* (I think, therefore I am). Another sign bears the motto made famous by La Pasionaria—Dolores Ibárurri, a hero of the Spanish Civil War—who said, "Better to die on your feet than live on your knees." Later I will hear that one of the murdered cartoonists quoted this line a few weeks before his death. The French newspaper *Le Monde* has called this "France's September 11," and one of the signs says simply, *01/07*. Another of the signs is a long list that starts, *Je suis Charlie. Je suis Abdul. Je suis Pierre....*

"We're all here together," I tell my granddaughter when she looks confused at the thousands around her, "so that everyone can know they're not alone. So we all know we're together and don't have to be afraid." I'm not sure if this message is for her or for me.

She has made *Je suis Charlie* signs for all the family to carry. "We talked about it in school," she says, "that people don't have to all be the same, that it's okay to be different." Her teachers also explained the concept of a minute of silence, then asked the children to bow their heads for one minute, which they did.

Over the next few days, I begin to hear from friends back in Canada; they acknowledge that yes, all this is terrible, but what about the two thousand Nigerians killed this same week by Boko Haram, why aren't we honouring those dead? Racism raises its head again. *Je suis Charlie,* they say from far away, is mere words.

But it's not. Not here, not now, when the fear and shock are stunningly real. Still, I begin to wonder; nothing justifies killing someone whose opinion you disagree with, nothing. But really, did those cartoonists go too far? I consider myself an open-minded person, but the cartoons I'd seen in *Charlie Hebdo*'s Christmas edition were shocking even to me, a non-Christian. Where do you draw the line, and how do you mark it?

The darker side of response now begins to surface in France with racist, overtly anti-Muslim, anti-Semitic and anti-immigrant comments, along with serious threats to mosques and synagogues. (I wonder "Why synagogues?" but no one else seems to notice this inconsistency. Or perhaps this piece of racism is so common, it's become invisible?) Thousands of French military and police have been called out to protect public buildings, including schools. Fear begets fear. Everywhere on the streets, we pass patrols of soldiers in groups of three, fingers on the triggers of their machine guns.

At a party one night, when I dare raise my concerns about *Charlie Hebdo*'s lack of moderation, a French woman snaps, "Political correctness!" and turns away, as if this is a distinctly North American weakness. And it turns out she's correct, at least from the French point of view. A lawyer in the group explains that "political correctness"—derogatory as that term is to some—marks a distinct focus on individual human rights that I now find out is more familiar, and apparently far more prized, in North America than in France.

His explanation helps explain my confusion over how these violent incidents seem at least as equated with French national pride and the right to freedom of speech, as they are with individual deaths. More than once in the demonstrations and marches, people have broken out singing *La Marseillaise*, the national anthem, and public statements seem to focus on *liberté* and *la République* rather than, say, decrying lawlessness and violence, as I'd have expected at home.

An article on January 8 in *The International New York Times* by Doreen Carvaial, and another on January 19 in *The New Yorker* by Adam Gopnik, help explain why the passion behind the French response seems focussed not so much on the violence committed, as on a magazine's right to satire. Both writers underline that what we call the "gentle" and "ironic" satire of North American political cartoons is nothing like what Gopnik, an American who lived for years in France, calls "a peculiarly French and savage tradition" practised for centuries by writers and caricaturists like Voltaire and Honoré Daumier. Throughout French history, he explains, under the rule of king and clergy, the only way to publicly protest without getting your head cut off was through satire. Satire, both these writers say—including or even especially the fierce satire of *Charlie Hebdo* that mocks Muslim, Christian, Jew, feminist, right and left, equally—represents a ferociously held defence of freedom of speech for the French in a way I, as a Canadian, find unfamiliar, even shocking.

Over time it's led to a serious clash of cultures because portrayals of the Prophet Muhammad are forbidden by most Muslim authorities, but caricatures—cartoons—are expressly forbidden. When John and I were in Turkey the previous year, mosques were stunningly decorated with tiles in an endless variety of colours and patterns, but unlike Christian churches where images of Jesus, Mary and other humans are ubiquitous, there was not a single human figure, let alone one of the Prophet Muhammad.

So I struggle with the breathtaking courage—or is it foolhardiness?—of the next issue of *Charlie Hebdo* that, with the help of staff from other French journals, comes out one week after the killings portraying the Prophet yet again, this time weeping and holding a sign that says, *Je suis Charlie,* with *Tout est pardonée* (All is forgiven) above his head.

Monday, January 12, 2015

I'm standing outside our granddaughter's school, waiting for her to gather her things when a small band of seven or eight kids walks solemnly past, crossing the school yard. Three hold *Je suis Charlie* signs. Eyes forward, they all look very serious except the smallest, who chatters excitedly, and another who shushes her after every few steps. This is serious, their small bodies say.

Five years later, on October 16, 2020, again in Paris, a high school teacher named Samuel Paty will be beheaded by an eighteen-year-old Islamic terrorist for showing his class the same caricatures of the Prophet Muhammad that had originally been published in the *Charlie Hebdo* magazine. Paty had been trying to explain to his civics students the French concept of *laïcité,* the French term for the separation of church and state, for the complete isolation of political and religious spheres—a key French concept that came into being as a result of the French Revolution. I only learn about this concept now, and don't pretend to thoroughly understand it. Even in France, there seems to be some confusion. According to newspaper reports, some take *laïcité* to mean freedom *of* religion—everyone's right to practice their own religion as long as it's kept separate from affairs of state. Others define it as freedom *from* religion, the absence of all religious symbols from public spaces, and freedom to say whatever you want, even about what others might consider sacred.

The French government took the killing of Mr. Paty as an attack on French values, specifically on *laïcité,* and declared Paty right to do what he did. But when teachers were later asked to talk to their students about the event, it was an extremely unsettling conversation, especially among Muslim students—and for

Muslim teachers. Some of the teachers, especially those in the poorer parts of French cities, pointed out that another reason for the difficulty of this conversation was that students raised the issue of yet another French principle, embodied in the French state motto of, "*Liberté, egalité, fraternité.*" Why should they defend *laïcité*, they challenged their teachers, if other state principles, especially of equality, are so missing in their lives, where they struggle with poverty and lack of jobs and opportunities?

A good question.

It's tempting to judge another country so distant, so culturally distinct from our own. When I got home to Canada a week after the *Charlie Hebdo* killings, the events of the past month wouldn't leave me. I'd thought—hoped, perhaps—that *Charlie Hebdo* and the related killings, as well as the intense religious and patriotic tension they evoked, were a "foreign" thing, separate from my safe Canadian experience. Haven't we historically prided ourselves on tolerance here, on a peaceful cultural mosaic? But then I remember that Canada too, has been touched by random horrors from those who violently disagreed with the status quo. In addition to the young soldier in Ottawa, in 1985 there was the bombing of Air India Flight 182, en route from Toronto to Mumbai that killed all 329 people on board, most of them Indo-Canadians. In 1970 it was the FLQ crisis, when the Deputy Premier of Quebec, Pierre Laporte, was kidnapped and murdered. And we've had our share of fire-bombings of bookstores and abortion clinics. Then there's the ongoing violence we've done to our First Nations peoples since Contact….

The violence in France raises (again) the question: How much respect for freedom of expression shall we—should we—

allow? Some say there is no difference between the violence of gunshots and bombs, and the violence of cultural suppression and racism. Or is there? Shortly after the *Charlie Hebdo* horror, Nova Scotia Supreme Court Judge Jamie Campbell, in his decision on NS Barristers' Society v. Trinity Western University, wrote in relation to a decision concerning sexual preference, "Unless tolerance engages the incomprehensible, the contemptible or the detestable, it is nothing much more than indifference."

So exactly how far do we let tolerance and freedom of speech go? How vigorously shall we defend it? In 2016 on the anniversary of the *Charlie Hebdo* shootings, PEN International, the group defending freedom of the press, affirmed, "the right to offend."

The debate over free speech and the right to differ is intense, global, vital. The children in the schoolyard were right; this is serious. And difficult. And it is becoming more intense.

For weeks after I got home from Paris that year, I cringed every time I heard a siren, but that experience, and reading later of the killing of the teacher, taught me I dare not be blinded by fear, including fear of the conversation itself. With all our differences, how shall we learn to handle fear and anger, to listen to those who are different, even our so-called enemies, how learn to link arms outside our usual comfort zones, as those leaders did in France? In this time of increasingly crude and violent responses at every level, how do we convene a respectful public debate on the questions crucial to each of us? How do we learn to listen, even when the conversations are difficult?

And what other option do we have?

Growing Golder

Love Letter

At a jazz club in Vancouver one night—audience packed tight—I noticed how the couple beside us had their hands on the table, fingers barely touching. They were in their mid-sixties, neither of them "beautiful" by the usual standards—a little overweight and dressed in unfashionable casual cottons. But whatever energy lived between them beamed as loud as the jazz piano on stage.

A few minutes later when I looked back, they were gazing lovingly across the table at each other, fingers now tightly interlaced. Just married? Doubtful. New "old" love? Possibly. During one slow jazz piece, their fingers danced with each other so erotically I had to look away.

And that's when my companion caught my eye. She and I too, were in our mid-sixties. Our husbands were out of town and this was "girls' night" at the club. She glanced at the couple and mouthed, "Cute!" I nodded.

But it got me thinking: Why is old love "cute"? Why not "hot"? Is it because younger people can't bear to think of older bodies engrossed in sexual pleasure, folds and flaps and fat and wrinkles glowing?

"Cute" is safer.

~

One day when I was twenty-one years old, eating lunch alone at a downtown diner, I'd noticed an older couple across the room from me. It was 1968, the early days of the Women's Movement in Canada. I'd just moved away from home and had been thinking about marriage—purely in the abstract, since I didn't even have a boyfriend at the time. About how it had been presented as inevitable for women my age because, "they" said, it brought you companionship, not to mention children, which at the time, I was very clear I didn't want.

I kept an eye on the older couple. In the entire time it took me to order, eat, pay and leave, they didn't say five words to each other. If theirs was "companionship," then from where I sat it looked totally boring. That day I vowed to myself that when—if—I ever got married, I'd always have something to say.

And I did. When I was dating, it led to some pretty one-sided conversations, especially when I met a man who was particularly quiet. But something kept drawing me back. John didn't "do" chatter, didn't speak unless he had something to say, and when he did, I listened because it was so—well—so to the point. At first his refusal to engage in small talk drove me crazy but in spite of, or maybe because of, his silence, I liked him. A lot. I liked his thoughtfulness, his insight, his lack of judgement. His quiet. And so we moved in together.

When we were still new together, apart from the necessary hours when we were at our separate work or other activities, he was almost always in my thoughts: What's he doing now? Is he okay? And very often: Has he forgotten about me yet, realized I am, after all, deadly dull and he's planning even now, how to break the news he's moving on?

By some miracle none of those nightmares came to pass and here we are, forty-seven years later. What happens after that length of time being intimate every day with the same person?

Someone once said cynically, "That's when you've got nothing left to say. You're bored."

Not necessarily. And I have learned that relationships are not always what they look like from the outside.

My husband still surprises me. After forty-seven years I still have moments of delight. When I was about to send the final manuscript of my first memoir of working as a carpenter to the publisher, John had just been appointed to a new, very responsible, very public position. In the book, as a young woman before I met him, I had recorded stories of a life that didn't always fit the image of a prominent person; I'd smoked dope, I'd slept with other men. The story of our early start as a couple is in there too, as is our messy breakup before we got back together for good, and married.

Before I mailed that final draft, I'd taken a deep breath and told him that if he didn't want to be this public in the world, I would withdraw the book. It was a very deep breath indeed—that book had been a long, painful twenty-five years in the making.

He read it, and said, "This book isn't just about you and me. This book honours working people," and gave it his blessing.

So no, I'm not bored with this man.

Instead, everything has become condensed between us. What used to feel like his inexplicable behaviour followed by long painful "relationship" conversations—always at my insistence, never his—with much drama on my part, are now mostly resolved with a look or a nod or a wry grin. We don't always like what the other has done or is doing, and there have been compromises (really, how important is it that the toothbrushes be kept on the left-hand side of the sink?) but we've come to accept this is just who we both are and we're not going to change each other in any of the big ways and really, none of the little ways either, no matter how much we wish it, or demand it, or wait for it.

For example, when the two of us first talked of marriage, I knew what I wanted; I wanted him to come home from work every night, throw his arms around me and tell me—again and again—how much he loved me.

I also knew this would never happen. My husband will never be like that. I knew the most I could expect would be that when he showed wild affection he might lightly touch my behind in passing. And I was smart enough to be clear that unless—until—I could accept that touch as a true measure of his love, his equivalent to throwing arms around me and loudly declaring his love (yet again), then I should not marry him.

I thought about it a lot, so it was a very conscious decision when I said, "Yes." I didn't give up my love of abundant and noisy affection, but I get it from my women friends, my family, from the children and animals in my life.

And sex? Yes, it changes over time, becomes less frequent, less sweaty. But it's there, and the intimacy of knowing this body, this flesh, so well for so long, is a pleasure that can only come with time.

One Friday night recently he came home from a week away and we watched a late-night murder mystery together. I don't usually watch anything more violent than nature programs on TV and as we got ready for bed I wondered aloud if the show would keep me awake. He laughed, "It's just a story!" and promptly fell asleep. But I couldn't sleep, kept thinking about the movie until I gave up, got up and went to sit in the living room thinking,

"There's a kind of freedom here." I caught a glimpse of myself as a woman so happy to have her husband home again, his sweet self, that she could even afford the luxury of fear, scaring herself with a movie late at night and now sitting in her living room sipping a Scotch, listening to the last of the revellers coming home from parties in the streets below, slowly drinking it in that he is here, he is home, in her bed. There is peace.

Things are much simpler now than in the early days of our relationship. Deeper. More secure. Often I don't think of him at all during the day, or only occasionally, in passing, or to send a quick text about whether he'd prefer fish or beef for supper when it's my turn to cook—like a small emotional pat to his absent backside. This person has seen me at my humiliating worst and still he loves me with a love like granite set in seabed. Storms now only settle our love deeper.

This is not to say there are not storms—there are. Or that there are not times I've been so angry I've thought of leaving him—again. More drama. But I trust utterly that sooner or later he will listen to the reasons for my anger. Sooner or later, we will arrange a time to talk, to work it out, sometimes with just a joke or a tease. Besides, I don't have energy for the histrionics of our early days. I don't need to. Now we can wait for each other, wait a long time if the other's not ready. And when the sea settles again, the silence between us is the silence of a calm night and a clear sky and looking straight up at a full moon as we lie on the grass holding hands. Not speaking.

I used to wonder if this reliance on another's presence is a weakness? He is my still point. How can I tell where I am if I don't have a still point to measure from? But here is love and familiarity and acceptance right beside me and I don't have to do anything but be grateful.

I'd heard of it before, spoken with scorn, of old people getting merely comfortable together, and once swore it would never happen to me. But here I am, doing it. Happily. He's now retired, but if John went away for a few days, I could always call up a woman friend. Maybe we could even go out and listen to music together at the local jazz club. I could, and did, enjoy a few days of spending time in my pyjamas, eating leftovers out of the pot, reading non-stop, all before the deep, quiet joy of his return, when I could say, "My partner is back."

Growing Golder

Forgot the name of the woman/man you were introduced to seconds ago? Check.

Sore knees? Sore hips? Check. Check.

Has that old question, "What do I want to do with my life?" recently rearranged itself into, "What do I want to do with the *rest* of my life?"

Then you're not alone.

When our parents retired from paid work at around age sixty-five, they usually eased into a life of coffee with friends and games of golf and bridge. But we, the "old" of the twenty-first century, have a problem; we're not finished. We're generally healthier and fitter than our parents and thanks to modern medicine, have a longer lifespan. So when we retire from our day jobs, we have plenty of other things to do. Just try making a date with another senior. "Sorry! I'm on my way to my cooking class/art lessons/yoga/you name it. Can we try for next week?"

~

Here's the problem; if I'm now retired and long past middle-aged (okay, say it, "Old!"), and into that category where not only do younger people give me their seat on the bus, but I'm happy to take it, then who am I now? When I was young, I was a carpenter, a feminist pioneer, an activist for women in trades. When I was middle-aged, I was a writer and teacher. I loved being—doing—all those things. But aside from writing these days, a largely solitary job made even more so for several years by Covid, what am I, who am I now?

Do any of us actually think we'll get old? I used to listen to my beloved senior aunties ask each other, first thing every morning, "How did you sleep, dear?" and think it an odd question. Now that I'm in my late seventies, I get it. A solid night's sleep (well, with only one or two trips to the bathroom) is a gift to be celebrated.

And there's that word, "Senior." Who *is* that, anyway? Passing the landmark age of sixty-five had some perks, like discounts on transit and theatres, an Old Age Pension. (Imagine a country where they pay you to be old!) But the other side of Senior is being no longer officially Adult. I figured that out when the young woman at the ferry terminal asked sweetly about my fare, "Will that be for a Senior or an Adult?" Gulp. I want to be both. I *am* both. Aren't I?

It hit me again one year on Remembrance Day, November 11. I was sixty-five at the time, singing at one of our choir's concerts in a local church. For the opening piece, choir members circled the pews and a handsome young tenor who happened to be close by, sang near my ear, "We shall remember them," and though I knew I was supposed to be thinking of those who died in wartime, I was instead reminded of my father who'd recently died peacefully, and my mother who'd just been diagnosed with a terminal illness. I wept. That's when it really struck me; one day, I too will die.

And I was afraid.

When I was in my thirties and forties, working in construction, I was afraid every day: afraid of not fitting in with the guys, afraid of being laid off, afraid of falling. But I always pushed through. As the men used to say, "Fake it 'til you make it." But after that choir moment I couldn't fake it anymore, and by age seventy, I had to admit my energy wasn't as great as it used to be, and my left knee was really hurting. "Pushing through," even with the help of massage and physio, was no longer an option. When I got honest with myself, I had to recognize that this life is a limited-time-only offer and though the expiry date may be unknown, the Big Layoff is 100 percent inevitable. At the same time, I understood American writer William Saroyan who at age seventy-two, on his deathbed mourned, "Everybody has got to die, but I always believed an exception would be made in my case."

It's about the body, and I'm not just talking about wrinkles. Friends call it FOF, Fading Organ Function, or GBC, General Body Crumble. When we get together these days, "How are you?" turns into what another friend calls, "The Organ Recital"—a growing list of everyone's latest medical misadventures.

Once—when I was looking to my mother for consolation after an alarming number of friends my age seemed to be getting serious illnesses and even dying—my mum, a woman of great compassion and sympathy, said only, "Get used to it."

So what to do? Panic? "Don't think about it," one friend said. But it's hard to avoid, especially in the middle of the night when my demons wake me and chatter doom. I need more time, more time…!

~

Certainly, in some traditional cultures including Indigenous ones, and in some churches, the name applied to us, this group of old guys, is Elder, which sounds a lot more honourable and distinguished than "old" or even "senior." Traditionally, Elders had and have a clear role to play in their communities; their job is to guide the younger ones. They're not just the group's memory but also its wisdom. It was Elders, First Nations and others, for example, who in December 2017 blocked a key road to stop the building of a gas pipeline in northern British Columbia. They showed up again in large numbers five years later to block old-growth logging at Fairy Creek, BC. They were the keepers of the land, they said, and the land and its gifts were in danger. Dr. Clarissa Pinkola Estés says in *How to Be an Elder: Myths and Stories of the Wise Woman Archetype* that Elders are the ones who "remember and tell, who record the stories for those who are younger."

But is this still true today? Especially, is it true in a non-Indigenous culture, which I am? Do young people even *want* our stories?

In a world where the focus is on power and beauty, on how much you produce, how much money you make and what you're "good for," how do we cope with the idea that inevitably every single one of us, no matter how rich or powerful or handsome, will become useless, even a burden, and yes, is going to die some day?

When I want to discuss this issue of "getting old," with friends, most seem loath to go there. They make a joke, dismiss it, change the subject. What's so scary about getting old? Well, there's the "getting closer to death" part, but lately I've also started to notice advantages.

"Advantages?" you ask. Yes. Why do we hear so little about the good parts of aging?

For one thing, I no longer care what anyone thinks of me; I have enough trust in myself, in my own judgement, that—within the limits of the law—I'll do what I want, the way I want to do it, looking the way I wish. I can now see how crippled I was as a young woman by what people might think of my looks, my clothes, my actions, etc. As a seventy-plus-year-old, I do and say exactly as I please. Sure, with a few more physical limitations, but still. If you don't like it—that's your problem.

During the days of Covid especially, it was a distinct advantage to be old, married, retired, and to have had the time to buy our own house, rather than to be young, dating, in a precariously low-paying job, and renting.

There are other good things, too. I've had the time to make a lot of mistakes and I've learned (mostly) the associated lessons. As Estés says, "An Elder wears the scar coat." There's a security that comes with that, a confidence from knowing what I know. Sure, sometimes this makes people my age a pain in the ass—some of us are a bit too liberal in handing out "what we know"—but we do know it.

"Wisdom" sounds pompous but that's the right word. When a young person says with perfect confidence, "I'm going to do this, then that," I may find myself nodding and smiling and wishing them every good fortune, but I know perfectly well there will be surprises and detours along their way because there were on mine, and on those of my senior friends. There's also no doubt that there's the same expression on my face that I could never read on my aunties' faces, of love and support, with a whisper of.... What was that? Knowing something they weren't telling, perhaps?

But of course, they couldn't tell, just as I can't tell now. What would I say? That "You might be surprised"? What would be the point? The enthusiasm, idealism and confidence of youth has my blessing, has all our blessings, because if the young didn't tackle every challenge with that kind of confidence, how would this world become a better place? I confess, I'm too tired these days to do it myself so isn't it great that the young are game? Even if I do know something they don't—that chances are close to 100 percent that it won't go entirely according to plan—it's okay. In the short run they might think the unexpected turns and dips are deeply disappointing, but they'll get it in the long run, and sometimes those unexpected turns lead to something even better than planned. That's wisdom.

There's another advantage to aging—and this one took me more time, and the leisure associated with a pandemic, to figure out. My body is fading, yes, so I've had to slow down. It was reluctantly done because I used to be notorious for being "busy," doing several things at once. But what happened as I grew older felt almost miraculous. I saw things! I mean, things I'd passed by a thousand times and yes, had looked at but never really *seen*. I never had time. Perhaps there's a sort of reason—someone once told me that ancient survival mechanisms dictate that when we're young, we don't need to notice "small stuff" because in ancient days, threat and danger only came from the unexpected and the moving—especially the fast-moving.

Aging means time to relax, to notice, to let the awareness seep in, to sit around the fire and think about things, really see things. "Boring!" I hear my young friends say, but that's the secret. It's not boring at all when you get here. Aging has forced me to slow down and heed things I never had time for before: the so-called "small" things like the swishy lullaby of leaves fingered by a light breeze, the cool hand of air across my neck on a hot day, sketches of an eagle circling against blue sky, the music of beach stones under my feet as I meander slowly, going nowhere in particular. I have *re*discovered things like the pure bliss of sitting, savouring chocolate ice cream.

~

What if I let go of the old me (who was once the young me) and see the new me? Not just the old and tired but the deeper me, the more genuine, the one who has shed her titles and is closer to the core.

There's a kind of wonder in getting older. There's the wisdom of being able to see and understand change—physical, emotional and intellectual. There's peace in it. We old codgers have learned empathy for others the hard way—by going through the changes ourselves.

As we get older—or as I first wrote, "golder," and hopefully that too—there's a sense of ease, of being able to take my time, of having time—at the same time as I know time is distinctly limited. Perhaps *because* time is limited. It hit me one day when I found out a close friend had just been diagnosed with Stage 4 breast cancer.

"There is no Stage 5," she said.

Sitting that close to mortality, to the loss of my friend, shook me, and I realized after, as I wept, that there really is no time for fear. Fear just gets in the way of seeing exactly what is here, now, in my life, in her life. What I need to focus on now is not fear or regret, or anger, or what *might* happen, but on gratitude that I'm still here now, here, with this friend, sharing these moments.

I want to *live* my life, all of it, not waste any of what remains on anger, fear, or regret. As we used to say in the old hippie days, "Go with the flow," or as the Buddhists say, "This is just the way it is." My intention these days is to be present, to pay close attention to what's going on around me—to *everything* going on around me, all the small miracles and marvels of nature and loved ones and friends. And to be grateful.

Don't Chicken Out, Chicken In!

I've always loved music but I've never wanted to sing solo. I listened and listen still to folk, jazz and classical music, and sang in choirs in elementary and high school. So why did I have this deep fear of singing solo even when choir directors and teachers said I had a good voice and excellent pitch, that I should try a solo?

No way, never!

~

Thirty years after finishing high school, after a move across the country and becoming a published writer and teacher of creative writing, I was going through a rough time. I don't know what made me think of music, but I asked several friends if they could recommend a good Vancouver choir. When several recommended the same one, I went to the next rehearsal. At that point, other than humming around the house, I hadn't sung for thirty years, but by the end of the first practice I realized I wasn't just singing—that was fun enough—or making harmony, the thing I love most about being an alto. Instead, as we sang, it felt as if every cell in my body was vibrating. My entire body was literally in harmony, aligned with the sixty or so other singers in the room in some glorious, utterly unexpected vibration.

I was hooked, and decided that to become a better singer I should take voice lessons. The teacher told me I had a certain gift, for which I thanked her. But a funny thing happened: everyone in the choir, my friends, my family, began to assume I would now want to sing solos. Why else, they said, would anyone take lessons? Because they're fun, I thought. Because I can hear my voice getting better and isn't that enough? But the people around me were so puzzled at my unwillingness to move to the next inevitable (to them) step, that I began to wonder if there was something wrong with me. I told myself I didn't want to sing solo because if I even imagined it, I began to sweat, my jaw clenched, my throat tightened, and a great slop of fear filled my belly.

Which was odd because by then I'd been teaching for fifteen years and teachers are performers, right? We stand at the front of a class and—to be frank—entertain students so they will enjoy what they're learning. Sure, I had butterflies for the first few terms but I came to love teaching—including the aspect of performance. "Show time!" I would announce to myself before each class.

As a writer, I also regularly "performed," standing in front of people to read what I'd written, often with musicians: bass, cello, guitar, even drums. Reading to an audience the words you've written in the deepest privacy of your own space is a bit like ripping your heart open in front of strangers and asking, *What do you think?* while they watch with a neutral if not (goddess forbid) distant expression.

Yet after the first couple of readings, it was no problem. In fact, I loved the feedback a live audience gives, not just after the reading when they confess what a certain poem or story meant to them, but even more, in the process of the reading itself when I can feel physically where a line holds an audience taut—and when it slips. This unspoken feedback, the body language of sighs and facial expression and laughter, as well as being able to hear the rhythm of my lines out loud as if through others' ears, quickly became my final test of whether a piece of work was finished. Often as I read to an audience, especially new work, I'd be making mental notes for revisions later, sometimes revising as I read. I loved doing readings.

And still I wouldn't, I couldn't, I didn't dare sing solo.

—

It became a mystery, even to me. Why didn't I just sing one damn solo and get it over with?

Then my husband, John, signed up for a one-week summer music camp so he could take guitar lessons. I don't play an instrument, but I *can* sing, so when I saw a class in the same camp on voice, I signed up for daily voice lessons, plus the camp choir. Fun!

It took a few years of returning to the camp, getting to know the regulars there, before I screwed up my courage. "Don't chicken out," someone advised, "chicken in!" And I signed up for a class for beginning performers. I knew we'd each have to sing at least once, alone, in front of the class, but what could be so awful in front of a chosen few who by then had become friends? Besides, I wanted to know why I was so afraid.

And I *was* afraid. I was terrified. The first morning of class, we all sang together. The second morning, we each sang twice, alone, a single line. I managed that, sweating. I hid among the singers around me. The teacher was gentle. It wasn't until the fifth and final morning that we each took our turn to stand up, alone, holding a microphone in our (trembling) hands and sang an entire song—a solo—to the tiny group in front of us, each of them also trembling (I assumed) as they waited for their turn at this torture.

I knew from voice lessons that the key to successful singing is to let your muscles relax, but when I stood up and took the microphone into my sweaty palm, I couldn't breathe. Chest, diaphragm, throat, shoulders, belly—I was suddenly a steel box from the waist up. Also, I was hyperventilating. By the time I finished one short chorus, I was panting and even *I* could hear my voice squeak. Where was all the richness of practice, richness I knew I was capable of in the privacy of the teacher's studio? Gone.

Still, I didn't actually have a heart attack and afterward, my audience was merciful, said I had "good tone," whatever that is. But the breakthrough—what felt most reassuring to me—was that all my fears were confirmed. Someone said, "Didn't it feel great after?" and I looked at her in confusion. No! It felt like I had just done a meaningless, terrifying, stupidly stressful thing and now it was mercifully over. I'd done it once and I never wanted to sing solo again. Ever! Case closed.

~

I guess poets "sing solo" but only in the process of creating the poem. Sitting alone, in glorious isolation in our rooms, we can let go of our small egos and open our hearts to whatever the Muse chooses to gift us with that day. We dare to explore what might be lurking in that image, that pinprick of attention we can't shake until we write about it.

When writers read or speak publicly, the creation is already done. Unlike singers, we're not making it up, not finding the right note on the spot, not recovering from a bad cold, not focused on relaxing with every syllable. Though delivery is an issue in making sure audiences can hear us, a writer's focus is on content, on the words, not on the breath with which the words are delivered. And after a reading or a class, I can return again to my private space, to quiet and blessed isolation—the *real* work.

In other words, the most vital processes of writing take place, at least for me, *alone* and *away* from people, while the essence of musical solos takes place *among* and *in front of* people. A writer is at heart a hermit, even if some of us choose to do our work in public caves like coffee shops and libraries. It's the work that matters, not the performance of the work.

I figure a musical soloist is at heart a social butterfly, loving to be the centre of attention—though there are exceptions. Pianist Glenn Gould detested performing—called his audiences "bloodthirsty mobs" and early in his career refused to do it, spending the rest of his life in the recording studio, if possible, at night. Perhaps this is why I chose to write a book about him.

As a writer I needed—no, craved—the long view, pondered and revised over and over until finally it became something solid under my fingers and only much later under my tongue. Musical soloists seem to want more, sooner. I'm deeply grateful for the nuances of audience response, but I read my work, take a bow and beat a rapid retreat. It's the work that matters, not the performing of the work. A musician may do a recording, but unless someone's there with a tape recorder, her/his live performance goes off into the ether. Writers seem to need to capture their vision, hold it down. We're zoo keepers. Twenty edits before it's read once, out loud, to an audience? No problem; twenty-five. Then hopefully, it's published, on paper.

So I was very clear, no solos.

Until one term, John's musical group couldn't find a vocalist. The group is all amateurs but they're serious musicians: piano, drums, cello, trumpet, guitar and bass. The teacher knew I'd taken voice lessons. Perhaps he'd consulted my teachers before asking John if I'd consider being the group vocalist?

I said No. No thank you, but definitely No.

As they got closer to the start date of the class and still couldn't find a singer, "We're desperate," the teacher said. Would I please, please reconsider?

Finally, on his third or fourth request, I thought: I'm seventy-seven years old. I'm terrified, sure, but if I don't defy my solo demons now, when will I? And it will help the group.

So I said yes, and in fear and trembling, went to the first practice. Luckily, I didn't record that practice because if I'd heard myself, I would never have gone back. It wasn't until two or three practices in, that I had the brilliant idea to record the sessions on my phone so I could practise better at home.

And I sounded awful! Was that really my voice, that tepid, bland, hardly discernable little warble?

I signed up again for voice lessons.

The teacher was great. In spite of past lessons, I was suddenly even more aware of how *physical* singing is, how sound has to power up from your diaphragm, through your chest to the live caverns of throat and mouth. I'd had no idea, or had forgotten, how vital the shape of throat and mouth are, where the tongue is, in a song's delivery. And what a difference it made, in the odd moments I remembered my lessons and focused all my physical attention on those never-before explored parts of my body!

Nonetheless, I was terrified before each weekly practice, as well as during. Theory and practice. It was like the old days of being a carpenter and knowing the theory of swinging a hammer, but then having to do it on the job with the strength and technique, hard enough, straight enough, to actually drive a spike.

Later, John would tell me that for that entire term I was a Nervous Nellie, as my mother would have said. I was distracted, impatient and hard to be around, always tired because I wasn't sleeping properly. I had my first-ever asthma attack the week before our final concert, no doubt at least partly stress-related. It helped that when a singer friend heard I was singing my first "gig" the next day, she advised me to "sing from my heart" and I instinctively knew that was a vital piece of information.

Then came The Day. I went into automatic. I knew audiences. I knew how to perform, how to act "as if" I was calm. Before the last of my four songs—almost finished!—I dared take a pause and talk to the audience.

"Yesterday I spoke with a friend who's going through a hard time," I told them. "She said maybe she just needed to break out of her same-old, same-old routines and do something different, and I said, 'Like sing your first-ever solo concert at the age of seventy-seven and finish up with *Fever*?'" She'd laughed.

"Something like that," she said.

So I told the audience I was dedicating this song to my friend Miriam, and I sang *Fever*. It was a song one of the members of my band ("my" band!) had asked us to do. Do you know it, that great old favourite sung by Peggy Lee and Ella Fitzgerald? "When you put your arms around me, I get a fever that's so hard to bear." If I was going to be outrageous and daring, why be halfway about it? So I sang it, the audience clapped, and I walked off the stage in a daze.

I'd done it—an entire set of songs, solo. The audience was kind, but I felt only numb. I could hardly talk as John and I headed home.

It wasn't until the next day that I sort of understood it. I had faced what is probably my worst fear and done it. Why had I been so afraid?

I suddenly remembered being in Grade 6 when my mother suggested I audition for the school drama group. I remembered the exact details of the classroom where auditions took place. It was a pale beige colour, with large maps of the Commonwealth around the walls. The desks—wooden chairs with an arm holding the front writing surface, a round hole for the ink well and a storage space beneath—had been pushed back to create a "stage," a space where auditioners stood. And I remembered perfectly how, the moment they called my name, I stood up, stricken with fear, and ran from the room. I never went back.

I have no idea what that was about, what childhood traumatic memory, perhaps, had just been triggered, but my fear of performing was there, even then.

~

The day after my solo debut, I actually thought about doing it again. It was sort of fun—I'm trying not to choke as I write that—having an audience, putting enough emotion, enough power into my voice that I could see it affect them. I had felt where my weaknesses were in that performance, and knew that with more work, more lessons, more practice, I could get better.

But when I told my sister about it, she said, "Are you insane? The whole time you were getting ready for this, you complained that you weren't writing!" And she was right. All my life I've tried my hand at anything that popped up, everything that got me curious. That's how I got into construction—curiosity plus being broke.

I'd taken on singing solo in the same spirit of "What's the worst that could happen?" but this time was a little different. This time I wasn't thirty years old. I was seventy-seven and life, as we all know, is a limited-time offer. I don't have a whole lot of time left and I have several books on the go. So my sister was right. I can't do both—sing solos and write—and I'm utterly clear that writing is my passion, my priority, my first love.

Now that it's over, I'm glad I did the thing I'd been so afraid of. I've learned a whole new respect for what it takes to be a singer: how physically engaging it is, how the harder a good singer works at it, the easier it looks. I will continue to listen to singers, now with more pleasure than ever that it's them doing this work, not me, and meanwhile I will appreciate more than ever the delights of writing in splendid isolation.

Over Our Heads

Attentus: to stretch toward, give heed to

To sit. Just that. With no intention or thought for when I rise, no leaning forward toward the next action, any action, any activity, any doing, accomplishment, busyness, involvement, diligence or hustle.

Does it make it any easier that as I make this promise to myself, I'm sitting in an aluminum deck chair on my narrow balcony four stories above a city street, blinded by the bright morning light around me? I have to almost physically hold myself back from action, any action. Surely I could make just a small cup of tea? A small pruning of this faded pansy in front of me?

I sit. A single crow calls. Another replies.

As a rising sun begins to clear the mist, sparrows twitter and hum, dash from tree to tree below and in front of me. Are they done with nesting? Busy with sparrow gossip, no more? Do birds too, make their early mornings a resting time?

A swallow glides by, calls. Of course, it must eat. We humans too. Even with the ingredients for breakfast waiting in the fridge behind me—what's the need to rush off? To rush, to spring, to race, to scamper, scurry, dash or even hustle to the next (self-) assigned task?

Red leaves fall on the deck from the tall maple on the street in front of me. One. Another. Slowly, the sidewalk is bejewelled.

I would never have noticed this small beauty if I hadn't been sitting. Still.

Cars zip by. The city begins to hum. And small birds sing over it all—a chorus, a choir that hallelujahs over the head of a single passerby. He's too busy, this one—running shoes and jogging pants—to notice.

Birds call. Leaves fall. And as if just waiting for the right moment, a single song sparrow dives from the blue above me, rises again, perches on the rail two feet in front of me, eye-level, and starts a small, feathered conversation.

Finally! she says. *You're paying attention!*

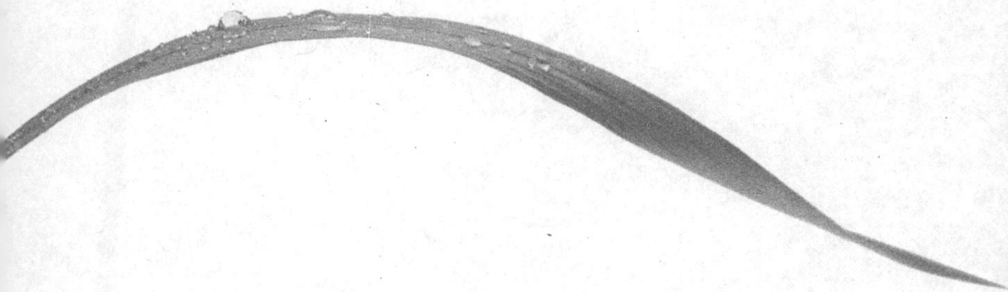

Notes

"Wonder Woman a.k.a. Emily Carr" was originally presented on a panel at the Convergence Conference in Nelson, BC, June 12–13, 2020. It's now available in slightly different form online at https://widespot.ca/writers/convergence-writers-weekend-2020-story-as-resistance/

"His Other Mother" was first published in slightly different form in *Nobody's Mother: Life Without Kids,* edited by Lynne Van Luven, Touchwood Editions, 2006.

"The Ear That Went Away" was first printed in *The Hearing Journal,* March 2024.

"Saying Hello to Fear" was first published in slightly different form in *Room* magazine, Issue 38.2, 2015.

Quote from Peter Levitt's "Pale Shadow" in "Honouring Why?" from *Within Within,* Black Moss Press, 2007.

"Seeking Home" was first published in slightly different form as "The Born-Here Immigrant" in *Going Some Place,* edited by Lynne Van Luven, Coteau Books, 2000.

References

Anne Cameron, *Dreamspeaker*, Harbour Publishing, Madeira Park, BC, 2005.

Clarissa Pinkola Estés, *Women Who Run With the Wolves: Myths and Stories of the Wild Woman Archetype*, Ballantine Books, New York, NY, 1992.

Clarissa Pinkola Estés, *How to Be an Elder: Myths and Stories of the Wise Woman Archetype*, Sounds True, Louisville, CO, 2012.

Jill Lepore, *The Secret History of Wonder Woman*, Knopf, New York, NY, 2014.

Kate Braid, *Emily Carr: Rebel Artist*, Dundurn Press, Toronto, ON, 2001.

Kate Braid, *A Well-Mannered Storm: The Glenn Gould Poems*, Caitlin Press, Qualicum Beach, BC, 2008.

Kate Braid, *Inward to the Bones: Georgia O'Keeffe's Journey with Emily Carr*, Caitlin Press, Qualicum Beach, BC, 2010. Originally published by Polestar Books, 1998.

Kate Braid, *To This Cedar Fountain*, Caitlin Press, Qualicum Beach, BC, 2012.

Moulton Marston, *The Adventures of Wonder Woman*, DC Comics, Burbank, CA, 1941.

Muriel Rukeyser, *The Life of Poetry*, 1968.

Robert Kroetsch, *The Lovely Treachery of Words*, 1989.

Robin Wall Kimmerer, *Braiding Sweetgrass: Indigenous Wisdom, Scientific Knowledge and the Teachings of Plants*, Milkweed Editions, Minneapolis, MN, 2013.

William Henry Hudson, *Green Mansions,* The Modern Library, New York, NY, 1927. Originally published in 1904, Duckworth & Co., UK. *Classics Illustrated* cover, No. 90, 1951.

Acknowledgements

I would like to acknowledge the many friends and writers who have encouraged and helped me over the years to write and hone these stories, most particularly our Pender Island writing group, The Muddy Lotus. ("No mud, no lotus" as the Thai Buddhist teacher Thich Nhat Hanh once said.) The Muddies include Andrea Spalding, Barbara Stowe, and especially Zoë Landale and Joy Thierry Llewellyn. Thanks to Vlad Konieczny and to Lynne Bowen, who started it all. Also, to Sandy Shreve for many years of love and support.

And I don't think I'd even be a writer without the ongoing publishing enthusiasm of Vici Johnstone and her trusty assistants at Caitlin Press, Sarah Corsie and Malaika Aleba. In these dire times for Canadian publishing, I bow to their commitment and hard work!

Also, my deepest thanks to Kevin, Alina and Zlata for their shelter and encouragement in France, and to Janet Fletcher and Art van Vliet for space and encouragement at a vital time. And what words can adequately express my profound love and gratitude to John?

I am also profoundly grateful to the Songhees, Esquimalt, W̱SÁNEĆ and Beecher Bay First Nations, for the privilege and joy of being able to live on their unceded territories.

Thank you all.

About the Author

Photo Eve Pollard

Kate Braid has been recognized in the writing community in Vancouver with an award as one of the Remarkable Women of the Arts, and with the Pandora's Collective BC Mentor's Award, and for poetry, the Pat Lowther and Vancity Book Prizes. She has also been writer-in-residence at Mabel Dodge Luhan House in Taos, New Mexico. Kate has written many books of poetry and creative non-fiction including two memoirs of her fifteen years as a carpenter, *Journeywoman: Swinging a Hammer in a Man's World*, and *Hammer & Nail: Notes of a Journeywoman*. She currently lives on Pender Island and in Victoria, BC.